Go Web Development Cookbook

Build full-stack web applications with Go

Arpit Aggarwal

BIRMINGHAM - MUMBAI

Go Web Development Cookbook

Commissioning Editor: Ashwin Nair
Acquisition Editor: Denim Pinto
Content Development Editor: Nikhil Borkar
Technical Editor: Jash Bavishi
Copy Editor: Safis Editing
Project Coordinator: Ulhas Kambali
Proofreader: Safis Editing
Indexer: Mariammal Chettiyar
Graphics: Tania Dutta
Production Coordinator: Aparna Bhagat

First published: April 2018

Production reference: 1200418

Published by Packt Publishing Ltd.
Livery Place
35 Livery Street
Birmingham
B3 2PB, UK.

ISBN 978-1-78728-674-0

www.packtpub.com

To my mother, Anita Aggarwal, and to the memory of my father, Anil Aggarwal,
for their sacrifices and for exemplifying the power of determination

`mapt.io`

Mapt is an online digital library that gives you full access to over 5,000 books and videos, as well as industry leading tools to help you plan your personal development and advance your career. For more information, please visit our website.

Why subscribe?

- Spend less time learning and more time coding with practical eBooks and Videos from over 4,000 industry professionals

- Improve your learning with Skill Plans built especially for you

- Get a free eBook or video every month

- Mapt is fully searchable

- Copy and paste, print, and bookmark content

PacktPub.com

Did you know that Packt offers eBook versions of every book published, with PDF and ePub files available? You can upgrade to the eBook version at `www.PacktPub.com` and as a print book customer, you are entitled to a discount on the eBook copy. Get in touch with us at `service@packtpub.com` for more details.

At `www.PacktPub.com`, you can also read a collection of free technical articles, sign up for a range of free newsletters, and receive exclusive discounts and offers on Packt books and eBooks.

Contributors

About the author

Arpit Aggarwal is a programmer with over 7 years of industry experience in software analysis, design, effort estimation, development, troubleshooting, testing, and supporting web applications. He is among the top contributors of StackOverflow with more than 9,000 reputation and more than 100 badges in multiple areas such as Java, Scala, Go, Spring, Spring-MVC, GiT, Angular, Unit Testing, Web Services, and Docker, and has written many technical articles for Java Code Geeks, System Code Geeks, Web Code Geeks, and DZone.

About the reviewer

Anshul Joshi is a data science professional with experience primarily in data munging, recommendation systems, predictive modeling, and distributed computing. He has worked on Spark and Hadoop ecosystems. He is a deep learning and AI enthusiast and holds degrees in computer science and data analytics. Most of the time, he can be caught exploring GitHub or trying anything new that he can get his hands on.

Packt is searching for authors like you

If you're interested in becoming an author for Packt, please visit `authors.packtpub.com` and apply today. We have worked with thousands of developers and tech professionals, just like you, to help them share their insight with the global tech community. You can make a general application, apply for a specific hot topic that we are recruiting an author for, or submit your own idea.

Table of Contents

Preface

Go is an open source programming language that is designed to scale and supports concurrency at the language level, which allows developers to write large concurrent web applications with ease.

From creating a web application to deploying it on AWS, this will be a one-stop guide to learn web development in Go. Whether you are new to programming or a professional developer, the book will get you up to speed on web development in Go.

The book will focus on writing modular code in Go and contains in-depth informative recipes building the base one step at a time. You will be taken through concepts and recipes such as creating a server, working with HTML Forms, session and error handling, SQL and NoSQL databases, Beego, creating and securing RESTful web services, creating, unit testing and debugging WebSockets, and creating Go Docker containers and deploying them on AWS.

By the end of the book, you will be able to apply your newly-learned skills in Go to create and explore web applications in any domain.

Who this book is for

This book is intended for developers who want to use Go to write large concurrent web applications. Readers with some familiarity with Go will find this book the most beneficial.

What this book covers

Chapter 1, *Creating Your First Server in Go*, explains how to write and interact with HTTP and TCP servers, optimize server responses with GZIP compression, and implement routing and logging in a Go web application.

Chapter 2, *Working with Templates, Static Files, and HTML Forms*, covers how to create HTML templates; serve static resources from the filesystem; create, read, and validate HTML Forms; and implement a simple user authentication for a Go web application.

Chapter 3, *Working with Sessions, Error Handling, and Caching in Go*, explores implementing HTTP sessions, HTTP cookies, error handling, and caching and managing HTTP sessions using Redis, which is required for a web application deployed across multiple data centers.

Chapter 4, *Writing and Consuming RESTful Web Services in Go*, explains how to write RESTful web services, version them, and create AngularJS with TypeScript 2, ReactJS, and VueJS clients to consume them.

Chapter 5, *Working with SQL and NoSQL Databases*, goes through implementing CRUD operations with MySQL and MongoDB databases in a Go web application.

Chapter 6, *Writing Microservices in Go Using Micro – a Microservice Toolkit*, focuses on writing and working with the Protocol Buffers, using a microservice discovery client such as Consul, writing microservices using Go Micro, and interacting with them through command line and web dashboard, along with implementing the API gateway pattern to access the microservices over the HTTP protocol.

Chapter 7, *Working with WebSocket in Go*, looks at writing a WebSocket server and its client as well as writing unit tests and debugging them using the GoLand IDE.

Chapter 8, *Working with the Go Web Application Framework - Beego*, familiarizes setting up the Beego project architecture, writing controllers, views, and filters, implementing caching backed with Redis, and monitoring and deploying the Beego application with Nginx.

Chapter 9, *Working with Go and Docker*, presents writing Docker images, creating Docker containers, user-defined Docker network, working with Docker Registry, and running a Go web application Docker container linked with another Docker container.

Chapter 10, *Securing a Go Web Application*, demonstrates creating server certificates and private keys using OpenSSL, moving an HTTP server to HTTPS, securing RESTful APIs with JSON Web Token (JWT), and preventing cross-site request forgery in Go web applications.

Chapter 11, *Deploying a Go Web App and Docker Containers to AWS*, discusses setting up an EC2 instance, interacting, and running a Go web application and a Go Docker container on it.

To get the most out of this book

Readers should possess basic knowledge of Go and have Go installed on the machine to execute the instructions and the code.

Download the example code files

You can download the example code files for this book from your account at
`www.packtpub.com`. If you purchased this book elsewhere, you can visit
`www.packtpub.com/support` and register to have the files emailed directly to you.

You can download the code files by following these steps:

1. Log in or register at `www.packtpub.com`.
2. Select the **SUPPORT** tab.
3. Click on **Code Downloads & Errata**.
4. Enter the name of the book in the **Search** box and follow the onscreen
   instructions.

Once the file is downloaded, please make sure that you unzip or extract the folder using the
latest version of:

- WinRAR/7-Zip for Windows
- Zipeg/iZip/UnRarX for Mac
- 7-Zip/PeaZip for Linux

The code bundle for the book is also hosted on GitHub at
`https://github.com/PacktPublishing/Go-Web-Development-Cookbook`. We also have
other code bundles from our rich catalog of books and videos available at `https://github.com/PacktPublishing/`. Check them out!

Download the color images

We also provide a PDF file that has color images of the screenshots/diagrams used in this
book. You can download it here:
`http://www.packtpub.com/sites/default/files/downloads/GoWebDevelopmentCookbook_ColorImages.pdf`.

Conventions used

There are a number of text conventions used throughout this book.

`CodeInText`: Indicates code words in text, database table names, folder names, filenames,
file extensions, pathnames, dummy URLs, user input, and Twitter handles. Here is an
example: "GZIP compression means sending the response to the client from the server in a
`.gzip` format rather than sending a plain response."

A block of code is set as follows:

```
for
{
  conn, err := listener.Accept()
  if err != nil
  {
    log.Fatal("Error accepting: ", err.Error())
  }
  log.Println(conn)
}
```

Any command-line input or output is written as follows:

```
$ go get github.com/gorilla/handlers
$ go get github.com/gorilla/mux
```

Bold: Indicates a new term, an important word, or words that you see onscreen. For example, words in menus or dialog boxes appear in the text like this. Here is an example: "AngularJS client page has an HTML form with **Id**, **FirstName**, and **LastName** fields as shown in the following screenshot."

 Warnings or important notes appear like this.

 Tips and tricks appear like this.

Sections

In this book, you will find several headings that appear frequently (*Getting ready, How to do it..., How it works..., There's more...*, and *See also*).

To give clear instructions on how to complete a recipe, use these sections as follows:

Getting ready

This section tells you what to expect in the recipe and describes how to set up any software or any preliminary settings required for the recipe.

How to do it...

This section contains the steps required to follow the recipe.

How it works...

This section usually consists of a detailed explanation of what happened in the previous section.

There's more...

This section consists of additional information about the recipe in order to make you more knowledgeable about the recipe.

See also

This section provides helpful links to other useful information for the recipe.

Get in touch

Feedback from our readers is always welcome.

General feedback: Email `feedback@packtpub.com` and mention the book title in the subject of your message. If you have questions about any aspect of this book, please email us at `questions@packtpub.com`.

Errata: Although we have taken every care to ensure the accuracy of our content, mistakes do happen. If you have found a mistake in this book, we would be grateful if you would report this to us. Please visit `www.packtpub.com/submit-errata`, selecting your book, clicking on the Errata Submission Form link, and entering the details.

Piracy: If you come across any illegal copies of our works in any form on the internet, we would be grateful if you would provide us with the location address or website name. Please contact us at `copyright@packtpub.com` with a link to the material.

If you are interested in becoming an author: If there is a topic that you have expertise in and you are interested in either writing or contributing to a book, please visit `authors.packtpub.com`.

Reviews

Please leave a review. Once you have read and used this book, why not leave a review on the site that you purchased it from? Potential readers can then see and use your unbiased opinion to make purchase decisions, we at Packt can understand what you think about our products, and our authors can see your feedback on their book. Thank you!

For more information about Packt, please visit `packtpub.com`.

Creating Your First Server in Go

1

In this chapter, we will cover the following recipes:

- Creating a simple HTTP server
- Implementing basic authentication on a simple HTTP server
- Optimizing HTTP server responses with GZIP compression
- Creating a simple TCP server
- Reading data from a TCP connection
- Writing data to a TCP connection
- Implementing HTTP request routing
- Implementing HTTP request routing using Gorilla Mux
- Logging HTTP requests

Introduction

Go was created to solve the problems that came with the new architecture of multi-core processors, creating high-performance networks that serve millions of requests and compute-intensive jobs. The idea behind Go was to increase productivity by enabling rapid prototyping, decreasing compile and build time, and enabling better dependency management.

Unlike most other programming languages, Go provides the `net/http` package, which is sufficient when creating HTTP clients and servers. This chapter will cover the creation of HTTP and TCP servers in Go.

We will start with some simple recipes to create an HTTP and TCP server and will gradually move to recipes that are more complex, where we implement basic authentication, optimize server responses, define multiple routes, and log HTTP requests. We will also cover concepts and keywords such as Go Handlers, Goroutines, and Gorilla – a web toolkit for Go.

Creating a simple HTTP server

As a programmer, if you have to create a simple HTTP server then you can easily write it using Go's net/http package, which we will be covering in this recipe.

How to do it...

In this recipe, we are going to create a simple HTTP server that will render **Hello World!** when we browse http://localhost:8080 or execute curl http://localhost:8080 from the command line. Perform the following steps:

1. Create http-server.go and copy the following content:

```go
package main
import
(
  "fmt"
  "log"
  "net/http"
)
const
(
  CONN_HOST = "localhost"
  CONN_PORT = "8080"
)
func helloWorld(w http.ResponseWriter, r *http.Request)
{
  fmt.Fprintf(w, "Hello World!")
}
func main()
{
  http.HandleFunc("/", helloWorld)
  err := http.ListenAndServe(CONN_HOST+":"+CONN_PORT, nil)
  if err != nil
  {
    log.Fatal("error starting http server : ", err)
```

```
        return
    }
}
```

2. Run the program with the following command:

```
$ go run http-server.go
```

How it works...

Once we run the program, an HTTP server will start locally listening on port 8080. Opening http://localhost:8080 in a browser will display **Hello World!** from the server, as shown in the following screenshot:

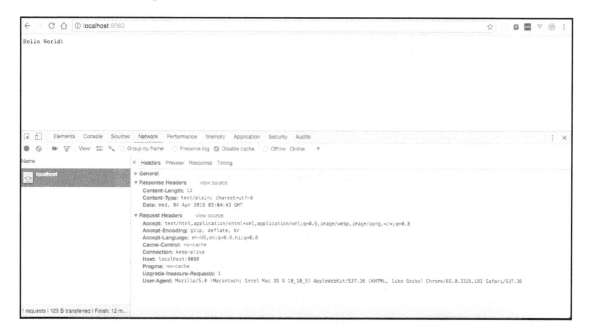

Hello World!

Let's understand what each line in the program means:

- `package main`: This defines the package name of the program.
- `import ( "fmt" "log" "net/http" )`: This is a preprocessor command that tells the Go compiler to include all files from `fmt`, `log`, and the `net/http` package.

- `const ( CONN_HOST = "localhost" CONN_PORT = "8080" )`: We declare constants in the Go program using the `const` keyword. Here we declared two constants—one is `CONN_HOST` with localhost as a value and another one is `CONN_PORT` with `8080` as a value.
- `func helloWorld(w http.ResponseWriter, r *http.Request) { fmt.Fprintf(w, "Hello World!") }`: This is a Go function that takes `ResponseWriter` and `Request` as an input and writes `Hello World!` on an HTTP response stream.

Next, we declared the `main()` method from where the program execution begins, as this method does a lot of things. Let's understand it line by line:

- `http.HandleFunc("/", helloWorld)`: Here, we are registering the `helloWorld` function with the `/` URL pattern using `HandleFunc` of the `net/http` package, which means `helloWorld` gets executed, passing `(http.ResponseWriter, *http.Request)` as a parameter to it whenever we access the HTTP URL with pattern `/`.
- `err := http.ListenAndServe(CONN_HOST+":"+CONN_PORT, nil)`: Here, we are calling `http.ListenAndServe` to serve HTTP requests that handle each incoming connection in a separate Goroutine. `ListenAndServe` accepts two parameters—server address and handler. Here, we are passing the server address as `localhost:8080` and handler as `nil`, which means we are asking the server to use `DefaultServeMux` as a handler.
- `if err != nil { log.Fatal("error starting http server : ", err) return}`: Here, we check whether there is a problem starting the server. If there is, then log the error and exit with a status code of `1`.

Implementing basic authentication on a simple HTTP server

Once you have created the HTTP server then you probably want to restrict resources from being accessed by a specific user, such as the administrator of an application. If so, then you can implement basic authentication on an HTTP server, which we will be covering in this recipe.

Getting ready

As we have already created an HTTP server in our previous recipe, we will just extend it to incorporate basic authentication.

How to do it...

In this recipe, we are going to update the HTTP server we created in the previous recipe by adding a `BasicAuth` function and modifying the `HandleFunc` to call it. Perform the following steps:

1. Create `http-server-basic-authentication.go` and copy the following content:

```
package main
import
(
  "crypto/subtle"
  "fmt"
  "log"
  "net/http"
)
const
(
  CONN_HOST = "localhost"
  CONN_PORT = "8080"
  ADMIN_USER = "admin"
  ADMIN_PASSWORD = "admin"
)
func helloWorld(w http.ResponseWriter, r *http.Request)
{
  fmt.Fprintf(w, "Hello World!")
}
func BasicAuth(handler http.HandlerFunc, realm string)
http.HandlerFunc {
  return func(w http.ResponseWriter, r *http.Request)
  {
    user, pass, ok := r.BasicAuth()
    if !ok || subtle.ConstantTimeCompare([]byte(user),
    []byte(ADMIN_USER)) !=
1||subtle.ConstantTimeCompare([]byte(pass),
    []byte(ADMIN_PASSWORD)) != 1
    {
      w.Header().Set("WWW-Authenticate", `Basic realm="`+realm+`"`)
      w.WriteHeader(401)
```

```
        w.Write([]byte("You are Unauthorized to access the
        application.\n"))
        return
      }
      handler(w, r)
    }
  }
}
func main()
{
    http.HandleFunc("/", BasicAuth(helloWorld, "Please enter your
    username and password"))
    err := http.ListenAndServe(CONN_HOST+":"+CONN_PORT, nil)
    if err != nil
    {
      log.Fatal("error starting http server : ", err)
      return
    }
}
```

2. Run the program with the following command:

```
$ go run http-server-basic-authentication.go
```

How it works...

Once we run the program, the HTTP server will start locally listening on port 8080.

Once the server starts, accessing `http://localhost:8080` in a browser will prompt you to enter a username and password. Providing it as `admin`, `admin` respectively will render **Hello World!** on the screen, and for every other combination of username and password it will render **You are Unauthorized to access the application**.

To access the server from the command line we have to provide the `--user` flag as part of the `curl` command, as follows:

```
$ curl --user admin:admin http://localhost:8080/
Hello World!
```

We can also access the server using a `base64` encoded token of `username:password`, which we can get from any website, such as `https://www.base64encode.org/`, and pass it as an authorization header in the `curl` command, as follows:

```
$ curl -i -H 'Authorization:Basic YWRtaW46YWRtaW4=' http://localhost:8080/

HTTP/1.1 200 OK
```

```
Date: Sat, 12 Aug 2017 12:02:51 GMT
Content-Length: 12
Content-Type: text/plain; charset=utf-8
Hello World!
```

Let's understand the change we introduced as part of this recipe:

- The `import` function adds an additional package, `crypto/subtle`, which we will use to compare the username and password from the user's entered credentials.
- Using the `const` function we defined two additional constants, `ADMIN_USER` and `ADMIN_PASSWORD`, which we will use while authenticating the user.
- Next, we declared a `BasicAuth()` method, which accepts two input parameters—a handler, which executes after the user is successfully authenticated, and realm, which returns `HandlerFunc`, as follows:

```
func BasicAuth(handler http.HandlerFunc, realm string)
http.HandlerFunc
{
  return func(w http.ResponseWriter, r *http.Request)
  {
    user, pass, ok := r.BasicAuth()
    if !ok || subtle.ConstantTimeCompare([]byte(user),
    []byte(ADMIN_USER)) != 1||subtle.ConstantTimeCompare
    ([]byte(pass),
    []byte(ADMIN_PASSWORD)) != 1
    {
      w.Header().Set("WWW-Authenticate", `Basic realm="`+realm+`"`)
      w.WriteHeader(401)
      w.Write([]byte("Unauthorized.\n"))
      return
    }
    handler(w, r)
  }
}
```

In the preceding handler, we first get the username and password provided in the request's authorization header using `r.BasicAuth()` then compare it to the constants declared in the program. If credentials match, then it returns the handler, otherwise it sets `WWW-Authenticate` along with a status code of `401` and writes `You are Unauthorized to access the application` on an HTTP response stream.

Finally, we introduced a change in the `main()` method to call `BasicAuth` from `HandleFunc`, as follows:

```
http.HandleFunc("/", BasicAuth(helloWorld, "Please enter your
username and password"))
```

We just pass a `BasicAuth` handler instead of `nil` or `DefaultServeMux` for handling all incoming requests with the URL pattern as `/`.

Optimizing HTTP server responses with GZIP compression

GZIP compression means sending the response to the client from the server in a `.gzip` format rather than sending a plain response and it's always a good practice to send compressed responses if a client/browser supports it.

By sending a compressed response we save network bandwidth and download time eventually rendering the page faster. What happens in GZIP compression is the browser sends a request header telling the server it accepts compressed content (`.gzip` and `.deflate`) and if the server has the capability to send the response in compressed form then sends it. If the server supports compression then it sets `Content-Encoding: gzip` as a response header, otherwise it sends a plain response back to the client, which clearly means asking for a compressed response is only a request by the browser and not a demand. We will be using Gorilla's handlers package to implement it in this recipe.

How to do it...

In this recipe, we are going to create an HTTP server with a single handler, which will write **Hello World!** on an HTTP response stream and use a Gorilla `CompressHandler` to send all the responses back to the client in the `.gzip` format. Perform the following steps:

1. To use Gorilla handlers, first we need to install the package using the `go get` command or copy it manually to `$GOPATH/src` or `$GOPATH`, as follows:

```
$ go get github.com/gorilla/handlers
```

2. Create `http-server-mux.go` and copy the following content:

```go
package main
import
(
  "io"
  "net/http"
  "github.com/gorilla/handlers"
)
const
(
  CONN_HOST = "localhost"
  CONN_PORT = "8080"
)
func helloWorld(w http.ResponseWriter, r *http.Request)
{
  io.WriteString(w, "Hello World!")
}
func main()
{
  mux := http.NewServeMux()
  mux.HandleFunc("/", helloWorld)
  err := http.ListenAndServe(CONN_HOST+":"+CONN_PORT,
  handlers.CompressHandler(mux))
  if err != nil
  {
    log.Fatal("error starting http server : ", err)
    return
  }
}
```

3. Run the program with the following command:

```
$ go run http-server-mux.go
```

How it works...

Once we run the program, the HTTP server will start locally listening on port 8080.

Opening `http://localhost:8080` in a browser will display **Hello World!** from the server with the **Content-Encoding** response header value **gzip**, as shown in the following screenshot:

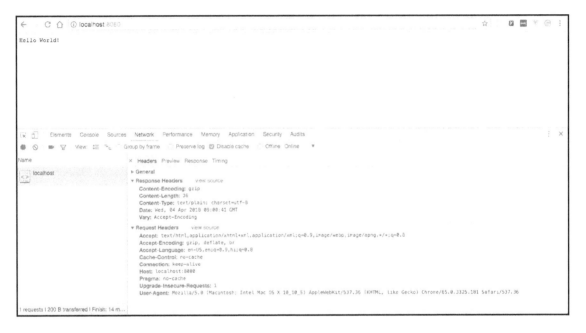

Hello World!

Let's understand what each line in the program means:

- `package main`: This defines the package name of the program.
- `import ( "io" "net/http" "github.com/gorilla/handlers" )`: This is a preprocessor command that tells the Go compiler to include all files from `io`, `net/http`, and the `github.com/gorilla/handlers` package.
- `const ( CONN_HOST = "localhost" CONN_PORT = "8080" )`: We declare constants in a Go program using the const keyword. Here, we declared two constants—one is `CONN_HOST` with a value of localhost and another is `CONN_PORT` with a value of 8080.

- `func helloWorld(w http.ResponseWriter, r *http.Request) {`
  `io.WriteString(w, "Hello World!")}`: This is a Go function that takes
  `ResponseWriter` and `Request` as input parameters and writes `Hello World!`
  on the HTTP response stream.

Next, we declared the `main()` method from where the program execution begins. As this
method does a lot of things, let's understand it line by line:

- `mux := http.NewServeMux()`: This allocates and returns a new HTTP request
  multiplexer (`ServeMux`), which matches the URL of each incoming request
  against a list of registered patterns and calls the handler for the pattern that most
  closely matches the URL. One of the benefits of using it is that the program has
  complete control over the handlers used with the server, although any handlers
  registered with the `DefaultServeMux` are ignored.
- `http.HandleFunc("/", helloWorld)`: Here, we are registering the
  `helloWorld` function with the `/` URL pattern using `HandleFunc` of the
  `net/http` package, which means `helloWorld` gets executed, passing
  `(http.ResponseWriter, *http.Request)` as a parameter to it whenever we
  access the HTTP URL with the `/` pattern.
- `err := http.ListenAndServe(CONN_HOST+":"+CONN_PORT,`
  `handlers.CompressHandler(mux))`: Here, we are calling
  `http.ListenAndServe` to serve HTTP requests that handle each incoming
  connection in a separate Goroutine for us. `ListenAndServe` accepts two
  parameters—server address and handler. Here, we are passing the server address
  as `localhost:8080` and handler as `CompressHandler`, which wraps our server
  with a `.gzip` handler to compress all responses in a `.gzip` format.
- `if err != nil { log.Fatal("error starting http server: ", err)`
  `return}`: Here, we check whether there is any problem in starting the server. If
  there is, then log the error and exit with a status code of 1.

Creating a simple TCP server

Whenever you have to build high performance oriented systems then writing a TCP server
is always the best choice over an HTTP server, as TCP sockets are less hefty than HTTP. Go
supports and provides a convenient way of writing TCP servers using a `net` package,
which we will be covering in this recipe.

How to do it...

In this recipe, we are going to create a simple TCP server that will accept a connection on `localhost:8080`. Perform the following steps:

1. Create `tcp-server.go` and copy the following content:

```go
package main
import
(
  "log"
  "net"
)
const
(
  CONN_HOST = "localhost"
  CONN_PORT = "8080"
  CONN_TYPE = "tcp"
)
func main()
{
  listener, err := net.Listen(CONN_TYPE, CONN_HOST+":"+CONN_PORT)
  if err != nil
  {
    log.Fatal("Error starting tcp server : ", err)
  }
  defer listener.Close()
  log.Println("Listening on " + CONN_HOST + ":" + CONN_PORT)
  for
  {
    conn, err := listener.Accept()
    if err != nil
    {
      log.Fatal("Error accepting: ", err.Error())
    }
    log.Println(conn)
  }
}
```

2. Run the program with the following command:

```
$ go run tcp-server.go
```

How it works...

Once we run the program, the TCP server will start locally listening on port `8080`.

Let's understand what each line in the program means:

- `package main`: This defines the package name of the program.
- `import ( "log" "net")`: This is a preprocessor command that tells the Go compiler to include all files from the `log` and `net` package.
- `const ( CONN_HOST = "localhost" CONN_PORT = "8080" CONN_TYPE = "tcp" )`: We declare constants in a Go program using the const keyword. Here, we declare three constants—one is `CONN_HOST` with a value of `localhost`, another one is `CONN_PORT` with a value as `8080`, and lastly `CONN_TYPE` with a value as `tcp`.

Next, we declared the `main()` method from where the program execution begins. As this method does a lot of things, let's understand it line by line:

- `listener, err := net.Listen(CONN_TYPE, CONN_HOST+":"+CONN_PORT)`: This creates a TCP server running on localhost at port `8080`.
- `if err != nil { log.Fatal("Error starting tcp server: ", err) }`: Here, we check if there is any problem in starting the TCP server. If there is, then log the error and exit with a status code of 1.
- `defer listener.Close()`: This defer statement closes a TCP socket listener when the application closes.

Next, we accept the incoming request to the TCP server in a constant loop, and if there are any errors in accepting the request, then we log it and exit; otherwise, we simply print the connection object on the server console, as follows:

```
for
{
  conn, err := listener.Accept()
  if err != nil
  {
    log.Fatal("Error accepting: ", err.Error())
  }
  log.Println(conn)
}
```

Reading data from a TCP connection

One of the most common scenarios in any application is the client interacting with the server. TCP is one of the most widely used protocols for this interaction. Go provides a convenient way to read incoming connection data through bufio implementing buffered Input/Output, which we will be covering in this recipe.

Getting ready...

As we have already created a TCP server in our previous recipe, we will update it to read data from incoming connections.

How to do it...

In this recipe, we are going to update the main() method to call a handleRequest method passing the connection object to read and print data on the server console. Perform the following steps:

1. Create tcp-server-read-data.go and copy the following content:

```
package main
import
(
  "bufio"
  "fmt"
  "log"
  "net"
)
const
(
  CONN_HOST = "localhost"
  CONN_PORT = "8080"
  CONN_TYPE = "tcp"
)
func main()
{
  listener, err := net.Listen(CONN_TYPE, CONN_HOST+":"+CONN_PORT)
  if err != nil
  {
    log.Fatal("Error starting tcp server : ", err)
  }
  defer listener.Close()
```

```
log.Println("Listening on " + CONN_HOST + ":" + CONN_PORT)
for
{
  conn, err := listener.Accept()
  if err != nil
  {
    log.Fatal("Error accepting: ", err.Error())
  }
  go handleRequest(conn)
}
}
func handleRequest(conn net.Conn)
{
  message, err := bufio.NewReader(conn).ReadString('\n')
  if err != nil
  {
    fmt.Println("Error reading:", err.Error())
  }
  fmt.Print("Message Received from the client: ", string(message))
  conn.Close()
}
```

2. Run the program with the following command:

```
$ go run tcp-server-read-data.go
```

How it works...

Once we run the program, the TCP server will start locally listening on port 8080.
Executing an echo command from the command line as follows will send a message to the
TCP server:

```
$ echo -n "Hello to TCP server\n" | nc localhost 8080
```

This apparently logs it to a server console, as shown in the following screenshot:

```
→  chapter-01 git:(master) ✗ go run tcp-server-read-data.go
2018/04/04 15:27:35 Listening on localhost:8080
Message Received from the client: Hello to TCP server
```

Let's understand the change we introduced in this recipe:

1. First, we called `handleRequest` from the `main()` method using the `go` keyword, which means we are invoking a function in a Goroutine, as follows:

```
func main()
{
  ...
  go handleRequest(conn)
  ...
}
```

2. Next, we defined the `handleRequest` function, which reads an incoming connection into the buffer until the first occurrence of \n and prints the message on the console. If there are any errors in reading the message then it prints the error message along with the error object and finally closes the connection, as follows:

```
func handleRequest(conn net.Conn)
{
  message, err := bufio.NewReader(conn).ReadString('\n')
  if err != nil
  {
    fmt.Println("Error reading:", err.Error())
  }
  fmt.Print("Message Received: ", string(message))
  conn.Close()
}
```

Writing data to a TCP connection

Another common, as well as important, scenario in any web application is to send the data back to the client or responding to the client. Go provides a convenient way to write a message on a connection as bytes, which we will be covering in this recipe.

Getting ready...

As we have already created a TCP server that reads incoming connection data in the previous recipe, we will just update it to write the message back to the client.

How to do it...

In this recipe, we are going to update the `handleRequest` method in the program to write data back to the client. Perform the following steps:

1. Create `tcp-server-write-data.go` and copy the following content:

```go
package main
import
(
  "bufio"
  "fmt"
  "log"
  "net"
)
const
(
  CONN_HOST = "localhost"
  CONN_PORT = "8080"
  CONN_TYPE = "tcp"
)
func main()
{
  listener, err := net.Listen(CONN_TYPE, CONN_HOST+":"+CONN_PORT)
  if err != nil
  {
    log.Fatal("Error starting tcp server : ", err)
  }
  defer listener.Close()
  log.Println("Listening on " + CONN_HOST + ":" + CONN_PORT)
  for
  {
    conn, err := listener.Accept()
    if err != nil
    {
      log.Fatal("Error accepting: ", err.Error())
    }
    go handleRequest(conn)
  }
}
func handleRequest(conn net.Conn)
{
  message, err := bufio.NewReader(conn).ReadString('\n')
  if err != nil
  {
    fmt.Println("Error reading: ", err.Error())
  }
```

```
        fmt.Print("Message Received:", string(message))
        conn.Write([]byte(message + "\n"))
        conn.Close()
    }
```

2. Run the program with the following command:

```
$ go run tcp-server-write-data.go
```

How it works...

Once we run the program, the TCP server will start locally listening on port 8080. Execute an echo command from the command line, as follows:

```
$ echo -n "Hello to TCP server\n" | nc localhost 8080
```

This will give us the following response from the server:

```
Hello to TCP server
```

Let's look at the changes we introduced in this recipe to write data to the client. Everything in handleRequest is exactly the same as in the previous recipe except we introduced a new line that writes data as a byte array to the connection, as follows:

```
func handleRequest(conn net.Conn)
{
  ...
  conn.Write([]byte(message + "\n"))
  ...
}
```

Implementing HTTP request routing

Most of the time, you have to define more than one URL route in a web application, which involves mapping the URL path to the handlers or resources. In this recipe, we will learn how we can implement it in Go.

How to do it...

In this recipe, we will define three routes, such as /, /login, and /logout along with their handlers. Perform the following steps:

1. Create http-server-basic-routing.go and copy the following content:

```go
package main
import
(
  "fmt"
  "log"
  "net/http"
)
const
(
  CONN_HOST = "localhost"
  CONN_PORT = "8080"
)
func helloWorld(w http.ResponseWriter, r *http.Request)
{
  fmt.Fprintf(w, "Hello World!")
}
func login(w http.ResponseWriter, r *http.Request)
{
  fmt.Fprintf(w, "Login Page!")
}
func logout(w http.ResponseWriter, r *http.Request)
{
  fmt.Fprintf(w, "Logout Page!")
}
func main()
{
  http.HandleFunc("/", helloWorld)
  http.HandleFunc("/login", login)
  http.HandleFunc("/logout", logout)
  err := http.ListenAndServe(CONN_HOST+":"+CONN_PORT, nil)
  if err != nil
  {
    log.Fatal("error starting http server : ", err)
    return
  }
}
```

2. Run the program with the following command:

```
$ go run http-server-basic-routing.go
```

How it works...

Once we run the program, the HTTP server will start locally listening on port 8080 and accessing `http://localhost:8080/`, `http://localhost:8080/login`, and `http://localhost:8080/logout` from a browser or command line will render the message defined in the corresponding handler definition. For example, execute `http://localhost:8080/` from the command line, as follows:

```
$ curl -X GET -i http://localhost:8080/
```

This will give us the following response from the server:

```
→  chapter-01 git:(master) curl -X GET -i http://localhost:8080/
HTTP/1.1 200 OK
Date: Wed, 04 Apr 2018 12:34:22 GMT
Content-Length: 12
Content-Type: text/plain; charset=utf-8

Hello World!
```

We could also execute `http://localhost:8080/login` from the command line as follows:

```
$ curl -X GET -i http://localhost:8080/login
```

This will give us the following response from the server:

```
→  chapter-01 git:(master) curl -X GET -i http://localhost:8080/login
HTTP/1.1 200 OK
Date: Wed, 04 Apr 2018 12:36:53 GMT
Content-Length: 11
Content-Type: text/plain; charset=utf-8

Login Page!
```

Let's understand the program we have written:

1. We started with defining three handlers or web resources, such as the following:

```
func helloWorld(w http.ResponseWriter, r *http.Request)
{
  fmt.Fprintf(w, "Hello World!")
}
func login(w http.ResponseWriter, r *http.Request)
{
  fmt.Fprintf(w, "Login Page!")
```

```
}
func logout(w http.ResponseWriter, r *http.Request)
{
  fmt.Fprintf(w, "Logout Page!")
}
```

Here, the `helloWorld` handler writes `Hello World!` on an HTTP response stream. In a similar way, login and logout handlers write `Login Page!` and `Logout Page!` on an HTTP response stream.

2. Next, we registered three URL paths—`/`, `/login`, and `/logout` with `DefaultServeMux` using `http.HandleFunc()`. If an incoming request URL pattern matches one of the registered paths, then the corresponding handler is called passing (`http.ResponseWriter, *http.Request`) as a parameter to it, as follows:

```
func main()
{
  http.HandleFunc("/", helloWorld)
  http.HandleFunc("/login", login)
  http.HandleFunc("/logout", logout)
  err := http.ListenAndServe(CONN_HOST+":"+CONN_PORT, nil)
  if err != nil
  {
    log.Fatal("error starting http server : ", err)
    return
  }
}
```

Implementing HTTP request routing using Gorilla Mux

Go's `net/http` package offers a lot of functionalities for URL routing of the HTTP requests. One thing it doesn't do very well is dynamic URL routing. Fortunately, we can achieve this with the `gorilla/mux` package, which we will be covering in this recipe.

How to do it...

In this recipe, we will use `gorilla/mux` to define a few routes, like we did in our previous recipe, along with their handlers or resources. As we have already seen in one of our previous recipes, to use external packages, first we have to install the package using the `go get` command or we have to copy it manually to `$GOPATH/src` or `$GOPATH`. We will do the same in the recipe as well. Perform the following steps:

1. Install `github.com/gorilla/mux` using the `go get` command, as follows:

   ```
   $ go get github.com/gorilla/mux
   ```

2. Create `http-server-gorilla-mux-routing.go` and copy the following content:

   ```go
   package main
   import
   (
     "net/http"
     "github.com/gorilla/mux"
   )
   const
   (
     CONN_HOST = "localhost"
     CONN_PORT = "8080"
   )
   var GetRequestHandler = http.HandlerFunc
   (
     func(w http.ResponseWriter, r *http.Request)
     {
       w.Write([]byte("Hello World!"))
     }
   )
   var PostRequestHandler = http.HandlerFunc
   (
     func(w http.ResponseWriter, r *http.Request)
     {
       w.Write([]byte("It's a Post Request!"))
     }
   )
   var PathVariableHandler = http.HandlerFunc
   (
     func(w http.ResponseWriter, r *http.Request)
     {
       vars := mux.Vars(r)
       name := vars["name"]
   ```

```
    w.Write([]byte("Hi " + name))
  }
)
func main()
{
  router := mux.NewRouter()
  router.Handle("/", GetRequestHandler).Methods("GET")
  router.Handle("/post", PostRequestHandler).Methods("POST")
  router.Handle("/hello/{name}",
  PathVariableHandler).Methods("GET", "PUT")
  http.ListenAndServe(CONN_HOST+":"+CONN_PORT, router)
}
```

3. Run the program with the following command:

```
$ go run http-server-gorilla-mux-routing.go
```

How it works...

Once we run the program, the HTTP server will start locally listening on port 8080, and accessing http://localhost:8080/, http://localhost:8080/post, and http://localhost:8080/hello/foo from a browser or command line will produce the message defined in the corresponding handler definition. For example, execute http://localhost:8080/ from the command line, as follows:

```
$ curl -X GET -i http://localhost:8080/
```

This will give us the following response from the server:

```
→  chapter-01 git:(master) curl -X GET -i http://localhost:8080/
HTTP/1.1 200 OK
Date: Wed, 04 Apr 2018 12:52:56 GMT
Content-Length: 12
Content-Type: text/plain; charset=utf-8

Hello World!
```

We could also execute http://localhost:8080/hello/foo from the command line, as follows:

```
$ curl -X GET -i http://localhost:8080/hello/foo
```

This will give us the following response from the server:

```
→  chapter-01 git:(master) curl -X GET -i http://localhost:8080/hello/foo
HTTP/1.1 200 OK
Date: Wed, 04 Apr 2018 12:54:03 GMT
Content-Length: 6
Content-Type: text/plain; charset=utf-8

Hi foo
```

Let's understand the code changes we made in this recipe:

1. First, we defined `GetRequestHandler` and `PostRequestHandler`, which simply write a message on an HTTP response stream, as follows:

```
var GetRequestHandler = http.HandlerFunc
(
  func(w http.ResponseWriter, r *http.Request)
  {
    w.Write([]byte("Hello World!"))
  }
)
var PostRequestHandler = http.HandlerFunc
(
  func(w http.ResponseWriter, r *http.Request)
  {
    w.Write([]byte("It's a Post Request!"))
  }
)
```

2. Next, we defined `PathVariableHandler`, which extracts request path variables, gets the value, and writes it to an HTTP response stream, as follows:

```
var PathVariableHandler = http.HandlerFunc
(
  func(w http.ResponseWriter, r *http.Request)
  {
    vars := mux.Vars(r)
    name := vars["name"]
    w.Write([]byte("Hi " + name))
  }
)
```

3. Then, we registered all these handlers with the `gorilla/mux` router and instantiated it, calling the `NewRouter()` handler of the mux router, as follows:

```
func main()
{
  router := mux.NewRouter()
  router.Handle("/", GetRequestHandler).Methods("GET")
  router.Handle("/post", PostCallHandler).Methods("POST")
  router.Handle("/hello/{name}", PathVariableHandler).
  Methods("GET", "PUT")
  http.ListenAndServe(CONN_HOST+":"+CONN_PORT, router)
}
```

Logging HTTP requests

Logging HTTP requests is always useful when troubleshooting a web application, so it's a good idea to log a request/response with a proper message and logging level. Go provides the `log` package, which can help us to implement logging in an application. However, in this recipe we will be using Gorilla logging handlers to implement it because the library offers more features such as logging in Apache Combined Log Format and Apache Common Log Format, which are not yet supported by the Go `log` package.

Getting Ready...

As we have already created an HTTP server and defined routes using Gorilla Mux in our previous recipe, we will update it to incorporate Gorilla logging handlers.

How to do it...

Let's implement logging using Gorilla handlers. Perform the following steps:

1. Install the `github.com/gorilla/handler` and `github.com/gorilla/mux` packages using the `go get` command, as follows:

```
$ go get github.com/gorilla/handlers
$ go get github.com/gorilla/mux
```

2. Create `http-server-request-logging.go` and copy the following content:

```go
package main
import
(
  "net/http"
  "os"
  "github.com/gorilla/handlers"
  "github.com/gorilla/mux"
)
const
(
  CONN_HOST = "localhost"
  CONN_PORT = "8080"
)
var GetRequestHandler = http.HandlerFunc
(
  func(w http.ResponseWriter, r *http.Request)
  {
    w.Write([]byte("Hello World!"))
  }
)
var PostRequestHandler = http.HandlerFunc
(
  func(w http.ResponseWriter, r *http.Request)
  {
    w.Write([]byte("It's a Post Request!"))
  }
)
var PathVariableHandler = http.HandlerFunc
(
  func(w http.ResponseWriter, r *http.Request)
  {
    vars := mux.Vars(r)
    name := vars["name"]
    w.Write([]byte("Hi " + name))
  }
)
func main()
{
  router := mux.NewRouter()
  router.Handle("/", handlers.LoggingHandler(os.Stdout,
  http.HandlerFunc(GetRequestHandler))).Methods("GET")
  logFile, err := os.OpenFile("server.log",
  os.O_WRONLY|os.O_CREATE|os.O_APPEND, 0666)
  if err != nil
  {
```

```
        log.Fatal("error starting http server : ", err)
        return
    }
    router.Handle("/post", handlers.LoggingHandler(logFile,
    PostRequestHandler)).Methods("POST")
    router.Handle("/hello/{name}",
    handlers.CombinedLoggingHandler(logFile,
    PathVariableHandler)).Methods("GET")
    http.ListenAndServe(CONN_HOST+":"+CONN_PORT, router)
}
```

3. Run the program, using the following command:

```
$ go run http-server-request-logging.go
```

How it works...

Once we run the program, the HTTP server will start locally listening on port 8080.

Execute a GET request from the command line, as follows:

```
$ curl -X GET -i http://localhost:8080/
```

This will log the request details in the server log in the Apache Common Log Format, as shown in the following screenshot:

```
→  chapter-01 git:(master) go run http-server-request-logging.go
127.0.0.1 - - [04/Apr/2018:15:14:13 +0530] "GET / HTTP/1.1" 200 12
127.0.0.1 - - [04/Apr/2018:15:14:20 +0530] "GET / HTTP/1.1" 200 12
```

We could also execute http://localhost:8080/hello/foo from the command line, as follows:

```
$ curl -X GET -i http://localhost:8080/hello/foo
```

This will log the request details in the `server.log` in the Apache Combined Log Format, as shown in the following screenshot:

```
127.0.0.1 - - [04/Apr/2018:18:45:41 +0530] "GET /hello/foo HTTP/1.1" 200 6 "" "curl/7.43.0"
127.0.0.1 - - [04/Apr/2018:18:45:47 +0530] "GET /hello/foo HTTP/1.1" 200 6 "" "curl/7.43.0"
~
~
~
~
~
~
~
~
~
~
~
~
~
~
~
~
~
~
~
~
~
~
~
~
~
~
~
~
~
~
~
~
~
~
~
~
~
~
~
"server.log" 2L, 184C
```

Let's understand what we have done in this recipe:

1. Firstly, we imported two additional packages, one is `os`, which we use to open a file. The other one is `github.com/gorilla/handlers`, which we use to import logging handlers for logging HTTP requests, as follows:

   ```
   import ( "net/http" "os" "github.com/gorilla/handlers"
   "github.com/gorilla/mux" )
   ```

2. Next, we modified the `main()` method. Using `router.Handle("/", handlers.LoggingHandler(os.Stdout, http.HandlerFunc(GetRequestHandler))).Methods("GET")`, we wrapped `GetRequestHandler` with a Gorilla logging handler, and passed a standard output stream as a writer to it, which means we are simply asking to log every request with the URL path / on the console in Apache Common Log Format.

3. Next, we create a new file named `server.log` in write-only mode, or we open it, if it already exists. If there is any error, then log it and exit with a status code of 1, as follows:

   ```
   logFile, err := os.OpenFile("server.log",
   os.O_WRONLY|os.O_CREATE|os.O_APPEND, 0666)
   if err != nil
   {
     log.Fatal("error starting http server : ", err)
     return
   }
   ```

4. Using `router.Handle("/post", handlers.LoggingHandler(logFile, PostRequestHandler)).Methods("POST")`, we wrapped `GetRequestHandler` with a Gorilla logging handler and passed the file as a writer to it, which means we are simply asking to log every request with the URL path `/post` in a file named `/hello/{name}` in Apache Common Log Format.

5. Using `router.Handle("/hello/{name}", handlers.CombinedLoggingHandler(logFile, PathVariableHandler)).Methods("GET")`, we wrapped `GetRequestHandler` with a Gorilla logging handler and passed the file as a writer to it, which means we are simply asking to log every request with the URL path `/hello/{name}` in a file named `server.log` in Apache Combined Log Format.

Working with Templates, Static Files, and HTML Forms

2

In this chapter, we will cover the following recipes:

- Creating your first template
- Serving static files over HTTP
- Serving static files over HTTP using Gorilla Mux
- Creating your first HTML form
- Reading your first HTML form
- Validating your first HTML form
- Uploading your first file

Introduction

Quite often, we would like to create HTML forms to get the information from a client in a specified format, upload files or folders to the server, and generate generic HTML templates, rather than repeating the same static text. With the knowledge of the concepts covered in this chapter, we will be able to implement all these functionalities efficiently in Go.

In this chapter, we will start with creating a basic template and then move on to serve static files, such as `.js`, `.css`, and `images` from a filesystem, and eventually create, read, and validate HTML forms and upload a file to the server.

Creating your first template

Templates allow us to define placeholders for dynamic content that can be replaced with the values at runtime by a template engine. They can then be transformed into an HTML file and sent to the client. Creating templates in Go is fairly easy using Go's `html/template` package, which we will be covering in this recipe.

How to do it...

In this recipe, we are going to create a `first-template.html` with a couple of placeholders whose value will be injected by the template engine at runtime. Perform the following steps:

1. Create `first-template.html` inside the `templates` directory by executing the following Unix command:

   $ mkdir templates && cd templates && touch first-template.html

2. Copy the following content to `first-template.html`:

   ```
   <html>
     <head>
       <meta charset="utf-8">
       <title>First Template</title>
       <link rel="stylesheet" href="/static/stylesheets/main.css">
     </head>
     <body>
       <h1>Hello {{.Name}}!</h1>
       Your Id is {{.Id}}
     </body>
   </html>
   ```

   The preceding template has two placeholders, `{{.Name}}` and `{{.Id}}`, whose values will be substituted or injected by the template engine at runtime.

3. Create `first-template.go`, where we will populate the values for the placeholders, generate an HTML as an output, and write it to the client, as follows:

```go
import
(
  "fmt"
  "html/template"
  "log"
  "net/http"
)
const
(
  CONN_HOST = "localhost"
  CONN_PORT = "8080"
)
type Person struct
{
  Id    string
  Name string
}
func renderTemplate(w http.ResponseWriter, r *http.Request)
{
  person := Person{Id: "1", Name: "Foo"}
  parsedTemplate, _ := template.ParseFiles("templates/
  first-template.html")
  err := parsedTemplate.Execute(w, person)
  if err != nil
  {
    log.Printf("Error occurred while executing the template
    or writing its output : ", err)
    return
  }
}
func main()
{
  http.HandleFunc("/", renderTemplate)
  err := http.ListenAndServe(CONN_HOST+":"+CONN_PORT, nil)
  if err != nil
  {
    log.Fatal("error starting http server : ", err)
    return
  }
}
```

With everything in place, the directory structure should look like the following:

4. Run the program with the following command:

```
$ go run first-template.go
```

How it works...

Once we run the program, the HTTP server will start locally listening on port 8080.

Browsing http://localhost:8080 will show us the **Hello Foo!** served by the template engine, as shown in the following screenshot:

Execute curl -X GET http://localhost:8080 from the command line as:

```
$ curl -X GET http://localhost:8080
```

This will result in the following response from the server:

```
→  chapter-02 git:(master) curl -X GET http://localhost:8080
<html>
<head>
  <meta charset="utf-8">
  <title>First Template</title>
  <link rel="stylesheet" href="/static/css/main.css">
</head>
<body>
  <h1>Hello Foo!</h1>
    Your Id is 1
</body>
</html>
```

Let's understand the Go program we have written:

- `type Person struct { Id string Name string }`: Here we define a `person` struct type that has `Id` and `Name` fields.

> The field name should begin with a capital letter in the type definition; otherwise, it will result in errors and will not be replaced in the template.

Next, we defined a `renderTemplate()` handler, which does a lot of things.

- `person := Person{Id: "1", Name: "Foo"}`: Here we are initializing a `person` struct type with `Id` as 1 and `Name` as `Foo`.
- `parsedTemplate, _ := template.ParseFiles("templates/first-template.html")`: Here we are calling `ParseFiles` of the `html/template` package, which creates a new template and parses the filename we pass as an input, which is `first-template.html`, in a templates directory. The resulting template will have the name and contents of the input file.
- `err := parsedTemplate.Execute(w, person)`: Here we are calling an `Execute` handler on a parsed template, which injects `person` data into the template, generates an HTML output, and writes it onto an HTTP response stream.
- `if err != nil {log.Printf("Error occurred while executing the template or writing its output : ", err) return }`: Here we check whether there are any problems while executing the template or writing its output on the response stream. If there are, then we log the error and exit with a status code of 1.

Serving static files over HTTP

While designing web applications, it's always a best practice to serve static resources, such as `.js`, `.css`, and `images` from the filesystem, or any **content delivery network (CDN)**, such as Akamai or Amazon CloudFront, rather than serving it from the web server. This is because all these types of files are static and do not need to be processed; so why should we put extra load on the server? Moreover, it helps to boost application performance, as all the requests for the static files will be served from external sources and therefore reduce the load on the server.

Go's `net/http` package is sufficient enough for serving static resources from the filesystem through `FileServer`, which we will be covering in this recipe.

Getting ready...

As we have already created a template in our previous recipe, we will just extend it to serve a static `.css` file from the `static/css` directory.

How to do it...

In this recipe, we are going to create a file server that will serve static resources from the filesystem. Perform the following steps:

1. Create `main.css` inside a `static/css` directory, as follows:

   ```
   $ mkdir static && cd static && mkdir css && cd css && touch
   main.css
   ```

2. Copy the following content to `main.css`:

   ```
   body {color: #00008B}
   ```

3. Create `serve-static-files.go`, where we will create `FileServer`, which will serve resources from the `static/css` directory present on the filesystem for all URL patterns with `/static`, as follows:

   ```
   package main
   import
   (
     "fmt"
     "html/template"
   ```

---

[42]

```go
  "log"
  "net/http"
)
const
(
  CONN_HOST = "localhost"
  CONN_PORT = "8080"
)
type Person struct
{
  Name string
  Age string
}
func renderTemplate(w http.ResponseWriter, r *http.Request)
{
  person := Person{Id: "1", Name: "Foo"}
  parsedTemplate, _ := template.ParseFiles("templates/
  first-template.html")
  err := parsedTemplate.Execute(w, person)
  if err != nil
  {
    log.Printf("Error occurred while executing the template
    or writing its output : ", err)
    return
  }
}
func main()
{
  fileServer := http.FileServer(http.Dir("static"))
  http.Handle("/static/", http.StripPrefix("/static/", fileServer))
  http.HandleFunc("/", renderTemplate)
  err := http.ListenAndServe(CONN_HOST+":"+CONN_PORT, nil)
  if err != nil
  {
    log.Fatal("error starting http server : ", err)
    return
  }
}
```

4. Update `first-template.html` (created in our previous recipe) to include `main.css` from the `static/css` directory:

```
<html>
  <head>
    <meta charset="utf-8">
    <title>First Template</title>
    <link rel="stylesheet" href="/static/css/main.css">
  </head>
  <body>
    <h1>Hello {{.Name}}!</h1>
    Your Id is {{.Id}}
  </body>
</html>
```

With everything in place, the directory structure should look like the following:

5. Run the program with the following command:

```
$ go run serve-static-files.go
```

How it works...

Once we run the program, the HTTP server will start locally listening on port 8080. Browsing `http://localhost:8080` will show us the same output we saw in our previous recipe, but this time the text color has changed from the default **black** to **blue**, as shown in the following image:

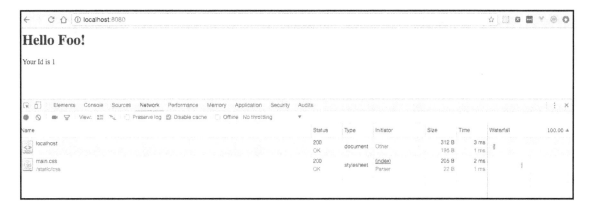

If we look at the **Network** tab of **Chrome DevTools**, we can see main.css, which has been loaded from the static/css directory present on the filesystem.

Let's understand the changes we introduced in the main() method as part of this recipe:

- fileServer := http.FileServer(http.Dir("static")): Here, we created a file server using the FileServer handler of the net/http package, which serves HTTP requests from the static directory present on the filesystem.

- http.Handle("/static/", http.StripPrefix("/static/", fileServer)): Here, we are registering the http.StripPrefix("/static/", fileServer) handler with the /static URL pattern using HandleFunc of the net/http package, which means http.StripPrefix("/static/", fileServer) gets executed and passes (http.ResponseWriter, *http.Request) as a parameter to it whenever we access the HTTP URL with the /static pattern.

- http.StripPrefix("/static/", fileServer): This returns a handler that serves HTTP requests by removing /static from the request URL's path and invokes the file server. StripPrefix handles a request for a path that doesn't begin with a prefix by replying with an HTTP 404.

Serving static files over HTTP using Gorilla Mux

In the previous recipe, we served `static` resources through Go's HTTP file server. In this recipe, we will look at how we can serve it through the Gorilla Mux router, which is also one of the most common ways of creating an HTTP router.

Getting ready...

As we have already created a template which serves `main.css` from the `static/css` directory present on the filesystem in our previous recipe, we will just update it to use the Gorilla Mux router.

How to do it...

1. Install the `github.com/gorilla/mux` package using the `go get` command, as follows:

   ```
   $ go get github.com/gorilla/mux
   ```

2. Create `serve-static-files-gorilla-mux.go`, where we will create a Gorilla Mux router instead of an HTTP `FileServer`, as follows:

   ```
   package main
   import
   (
     "html/template"
     "log"
     "net/http"
     "github.com/gorilla/mux"
   )
   const
   (
     CONN_HOST = "localhost"
     CONN_PORT = "8080"
   )
   type Person struct
   {
     Id string
     Name string
   }
   ```

```go
func renderTemplate(w http.ResponseWriter, r *http.Request)
{
  person := Person{Id: "1", Name: "Foo"}
  parsedTemplate, _ := template.ParseFiles("templates/
  first-template.html")
  err := parsedTemplate.Execute(w, person)
  if err != nil
  {
    log.Printf("Error occurred while executing the template
    or writing its output : ", err)
    return
  }
}
func main()
{
  router := mux.NewRouter()
  router.HandleFunc("/", renderTemplate).Methods("GET")
  router.PathPrefix("/").Handler(http.StripPrefix("/static",
  http.FileServer(http.Dir("static/"))))
  err := http.ListenAndServe(CONN_HOST+":"+CONN_PORT, router)
  if err != nil
  {
    log.Fatal("error starting http server : ", err)
    return
  }
}
```

3. Run the program with the following command:

```
$ go run serve-static-files-gorilla-mux.go
```

How it works...

Once we run the program, the HTTP server will start locally listening on port 8080.

Browsing `http://localhost:8080` will show us the same output we saw in our previous recipe, as shown in the following screenshot:

Let's understand the changes we introduced in the `main()` method as part of this recipe:

- `router :=mux.NewRouter()`: Here we instantiated the `gorilla/mux` router calling the `NewRouter()` handler of the mux router.
- `router.HandleFunc("/",renderTemplate).Methods("GET")`: Here we registered the `/` URL pattern with the `renderTemplate` handler. This means `renderTemplate` will execute for every request with the URL pattern `/`.
- `router.PathPrefix("/").Handler(http.StripPrefix("/static", http.FileServer(http.Dir("static/"))))`: Here we are registering `/` as a new route along with setting the handler to be executed once it is called.
- `http.StripPrefix("/static", http.FileServer(http.Dir("static/")))`: This returns a handler that serves HTTP requests by removing `/static` from the request URL's path and invoking the file server. `StripPrefix` handles a request for a path that doesn't begin with a prefix by replying with an HTTP 404.

Creating your first HTML form

Whenever we want to collect the data from the client and send it to the server for processing, implementing an HTML form is the best choice. We will be covering this in this recipe.

How to do it...

In this recipe, we will create a simple HTML form that has two input fields and a button to submit the form. Perform the following steps:

1. Create `login-form.html` inside the `templates` directory, as follows:

   ```
   $ mkdir templates && cd templates && touch login-form.html
   ```

2. Copy the following content to `login-form.html`:

   ```html
   <html>
     <head>
       <title>First Form</title>
     </head>
     <body>
       <h1>Login</h1>
       <form method="post" action="/login">
         <label for="username">Username</label>
         <input type="text" id="username" name="username">
         <label for="password">Password</label>
         <input type="password" id="password" name="password">
         <button type="submit">Login</button>
       </form>
     </body>
   </html>
   ```

   The preceding template has two textboxes—`username` and `password`—along with a **Login** button.

   On clicking the **Login** button, the client will make a `POST` call to an action defined in an HTML form, which is `/login` in our case.

3. Create `html-form.go`, where we will parse the form template and write it onto an HTTP response stream, as follows:

   ```go
   package main
   import
   (
     "html/template"
     "log"
     "net/http"
   )
   const
   (
     CONN_HOST = "localhost"
   ```

```
  CONN_PORT = "8080"
)
func login(w http.ResponseWriter, r *http.Request)
{
  parsedTemplate, _ := template.ParseFiles("templates/
  login-form.html")
  parsedTemplate.Execute(w, nil)
}
func main()
{
  http.HandleFunc("/", login)
  err := http.ListenAndServe(CONN_HOST+":"+CONN_PORT, nil)
  if err != nil
  {
    log.Fatal("error starting http server : ", err)
    return
  }
}
```

With everything in place, the directory structure should look like the following:

4. Run the program with the following command:

```
$ go run html-form.go
```

How it works...

Once we run the program, the HTTP server will start locally listening on port 8080. Browsing http://localhost:8080 will show us an HTML form, as shown in the following screenshot:

Let's understand the program we have written:

- func login(w http.ResponseWriter, r *http.Request) { parsedTemplate, _ := template.ParseFiles("templates/login-form.html") parsedTemplate.Execute(w, nil) }: This is a Go function that accepts ResponseWriter and Request as input parameters, parses login-form.html, and returns a new template.

- http.HandleFunc("/", login): Here we are registering a login function with the / URL pattern using HandleFunc of the net/http package, which means the login function gets executed every time we access the HTTP URL with the / pattern passing ResponseWriter and Request as the parameters to it.

- err := http.ListenAndServe(CONN_HOST+":"+CONN_PORT, nil): Here we are calling http.ListenAndServe to serve HTTP requests that handle each incoming connection in a separate Goroutine. ListenAndServe accepts two parameters—the server address and the handler—where the server address is localhost:8080 and the handler is nil.

- if err != nil { log.Fatal("error starting http server : ", err) return}: Here we check if there is a problem with starting the server. If there is, then log the error and exit with a status code of 1.

Reading your first HTML form

Once an HTML form is submitted, we have to read the client data on the server side to take an appropriate action. We will be covering this in this recipe.

Getting ready...

Since we have already created an HTML form in our previous recipe, we will just extend the recipe to read its field values.

How to do it...

1. Install the `github.com/gorilla/schema` package using the `go get` command, as follows:

   ```
   $ go get github.com/gorilla/schema
   ```

2. Create `html-form-read.go`, where we will read an HTML form field after decoding it using the `github.com/gorilla/schema` package and write **Hello** followed by the username to an HTTP response stream, as follows:

   ```
   package main
   import
   (
     "fmt"
     "html/template"
     "log"
     "net/http"
     "github.com/gorilla/schema"
   )
   const
   (
     CONN_HOST = "localhost"
     CONN_PORT = "8080"
   )
   type User struct
   {
     Username string
     Password string
   }
   func readForm(r *http.Request) *User
   {
   ```

```
  r.ParseForm()
  user := new(User)
  decoder := schema.NewDecoder()
  decodeErr := decoder.Decode(user, r.PostForm)
  if decodeErr != nil
  {
    log.Printf("error mapping parsed form data to struct : ",
    decodeErr)
  }
  return user
}
func login(w http.ResponseWriter, r *http.Request)
{
  if r.Method == "GET"
  {
    parsedTemplate, _ := template.ParseFiles("templates/
    login-form.html")
    parsedTemplate.Execute(w, nil)
  }
  else
  {
    user := readForm(r)
    fmt.Fprintf(w, "Hello "+user.Username+"!")
  }
}
func main()
{
  http.HandleFunc("/", login)
  err := http.ListenAndServe(CONN_HOST+":"+CONN_PORT, nil)
  if err != nil
  {
    log.Fatal("error starting http server : ", err)
    return
  }
}
```

3. Run the program with the following command:

```
$ go run html-form-read.go
```

How it works...

Once we run the program, the HTTP server will start locally listening on port 8080. Browsing `http://localhost:8080` will show us an HTML form, as shown in the following screenshot:

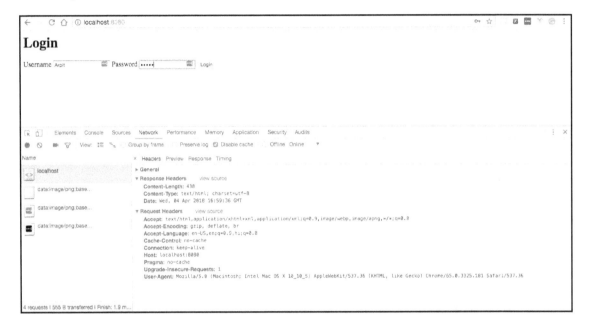

Once we enter the username and password and click on the **Login** button, we will see **Hello** followed by the username as the response from the server, as shown in the following screenshot:

Let's understand the changes we introduced as part of this recipe:

1. Using `import ( "fmt" "html/template" "log" "net/http" "github.com/gorilla/schema")`, we imported two additional packages—fmt and `github.com/gorilla/schema`—which help to convert `struct`s to and from `Form` values.

2. Next, we defined the `User struct` type, which has `Username` and `Password` fields, as follows:

```
type User struct
{
  Username string
  Password string
}
```

3. Then, we defined the readForm handler, which takes HTTP Request as an input parameter and returns User, as follows:

```
func readForm(r *http.Request) *User {
 r.ParseForm()
 user := new(User)
 decoder := schema.NewDecoder()
 decodeErr := decoder.Decode(user, r.PostForm)
 if decodeErr != nil {
 log.Printf("error mapping parsed form data to struct : ",
 decodeErr)
 }
 return user
 }
```

Let's understand this Go function in detail:

- r.ParseForm(): Here we parse the request body as a form and put the results into both r.PostForm and r.Form.
- user := new(User): Here we create a new User struct type.
- decoder := schema.NewDecoder(): Here we are creating a decoder, which we will be using to fill a user struct with Form values.
- decodeErr := decoder.Decode(user, r.PostForm): Here we decode parsed form data from POST body parameters to a user struct.

> r.PostForm is only available after ParseForm is called.

- if decodeErr != nil { log.Printf("error mapping parsed form data to struct : ", decodeErr) }: Here we check whether there is any problem with mapping form data to a struct. If there is, then log it.

Then, we defined a login handler, which checks if the HTTP request calling the handler is a GET request and then parses login-form.html from the templates directory and writes it to an HTTP response stream; otherwise, it calls the readForm handler, as follows:

```
func login(w http.ResponseWriter, r *http.Request)
{
  if r.Method == "GET"
  {
    parsedTemplate, _ := template.ParseFiles("templates/
    login-form.html")
```

```
    parsedTemplate.Execute(w, nil)
  }
  else
  {
    user := readForm(r)
    fmt.Fprintf(w, "Hello "+user.Username+"!")
  }
}
```

Validating your first HTML form

Most of the time, we have to validate a client's input before processing it, which can be achieved through the number of external packages in Go, such as gopkg.in/go-playground/validator.v9, gopkg.in/validator.v2, and github.com/asaskevich/govalidator.

In this recipe, we will be working with the most famous and commonly used validator, github.com/asaskevich/govalidator, to validate our HTML form.

Getting ready...

As we have already created and read an HTML form in our previous recipe, we will just extend it to validate its field values.

How to do it...

1. Install github.com/asaskevich/govalidator and the github.com/gorilla/schema package using the go get command, as follows:

    ```
    $ go get github.com/asaskevich/govalidator
    $ go get github.com/gorilla/schema
    ```

2. Create `html-form-validation.go`, where we will read an HTML form, decode it using `github.com/gorilla/schema`, and validate each field of it against a tag defined in the `User struct` using `github.com/asaskevich/govalidator`, as follows:

```
package main
import
(
  "fmt"
  "html/template"
  "log"
  "net/http"
  "github.com/asaskevich/govalidator"
  "github.com/gorilla/schema"
)
const
(
  CONN_HOST = "localhost"
  CONN_PORT = "8080"
  USERNAME_ERROR_MESSAGE = "Please enter a valid Username"
  PASSWORD_ERROR_MESSAGE = "Please enter a valid Password"
  GENERIC_ERROR_MESSAGE = "Validation Error"
)
type User struct
{
  Username string `valid:"alpha,required"`
  Password string `valid:"alpha,required"`
}
func readForm(r *http.Request) *User
{
  r.ParseForm()
  user := new(User)
  decoder := schema.NewDecoder()
  decodeErr := decoder.Decode(user, r.PostForm)
  if decodeErr != nil
  {
    log.Printf("error mapping parsed form data to struct : ",
    decodeErr)
  }
  return user
}
func validateUser(w http.ResponseWriter, r *http.Request, user
*User) (bool, string)
{
  valid, validationError := govalidator.ValidateStruct(user)
  if !valid
  {
```

```
  usernameError := govalidator.ErrorByField(validationError,
  "Username")
  passwordError := govalidator.ErrorByField(validationError,
  "Password")
  if usernameError != ""
  {
    log.Printf("username validation error : ", usernameError)
    return valid, USERNAME_ERROR_MESSAGE
  }
  if passwordError != ""
  {
    log.Printf("password validation error : ", passwordError)
    return valid, PASSWORD_ERROR_MESSAGE
  }
  }
  return valid, GENERIC_ERROR_MESSAGE
}
func login(w http.ResponseWriter, r *http.Request)
{
  if r.Method == "GET"
  {
    parsedTemplate, _ := template.ParseFiles("templates/
    login-form.html")
    parsedTemplate.Execute(w, nil)
  }
  else
  {
    user := readForm(r)
    valid, validationErrorMessage := validateUser(w, r, user)
    if !valid
    {
      fmt.Fprintf(w, validationErrorMessage)
      return
    }
    fmt.Fprintf(w, "Hello "+user.Username+"!")
  }
}
func main()
{
  http.HandleFunc("/", login)
  err := http.ListenAndServe(CONN_HOST+":"+CONN_PORT, nil)
  if err != nil
  {
    log.Fatal("error starting http server : ", err)
    return
  }
}
```

3. Run the program with the following command:

```
$ go run html-form-validation.go
```

How it works...

Once we run the program, the HTTP server will start locally listening on port 8080. Browsing `http://localhost:8080` will show us an HTML form, as shown in the following screenshot:

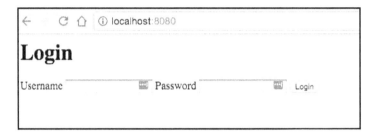

Then submit the form with the valid values:

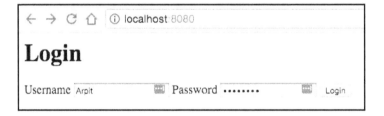

It will show us the **Hello** followed by the username on a browser screen, as shown in the following screenshot:

Submitting the form with the value as non-alpha in any of the fields will show us the error message. For example, submitting the form with the **Username** value as 1234:

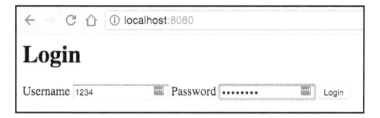

It will show us an error message on the browser, as shown in the following screenshot:

Moreover, we can submit an HTML form from the command line as:

```
$ curl --data "username=Foo&password=password" http://localhost:8080/
```

This will give us the same output that we get in the browser:

```
→  ~ curl --data "username=Arpit&password=password" http://localhost:8080/
Hello Arpit!
```

Let's understand the change we introduced in this recipe:

1. Using import ("fmt", "html/template", "log", "net/http" "github.com/asaskevich/govalidator" "github.com/gorilla/schema"), we imported an additional package—github.com/asaskevich/govalidator, which helps us to validate structs.

2. Next, we updated the `User struct` type to include a string literal tag with the key as `valid` and `value` as `alpha, required`, as follows:

```
type User struct
{
  Username string `valid:"alpha,required"`
  Password string
  valid:"alpha,required"
}
```

3. Next, we defined a `validateUser` handler, which takes `ResponseWriter`, `Request`, and `User` as inputs and returns a `bool` and `string`, which are the struct valid status and validation error message respectively. In this handler, we validated struct tags calling the `ValidateStruct` handler from `govalidator`. If there is an error in validating the field, then we fetch the error calling the `ErrorByField` handler from `govalidator` and return the result along with the validation error message.

4. Next, we updated the `login` handler to call `validateUser` passing (`w http.ResponseWriter, r *http.Request, user *User`) as input parameters to it and check for any validation errors. If there are errors, then we write an error message to an HTTP response stream and return it.

Uploading your first file

One of the most common scenarios in any web application is uploading a file or a folder to the server. For example, if we are developing a job portal, then we may have to provide an option where the applicant can upload their profile/resume, or, let's say, we have to develop an e-commerce website with a feature where the customer can upload their orders in bulk using a file.

Achieving the functionality to upload a file in Go is quite easy using its built-in packages, which we will be covering in this recipe.

How to do it...

In this recipe, we are going to create an HTML form with a field of type file, which lets the user pick one or more files to upload to a server via a form submission. Perform the following steps:

1. Create upload-file.html inside the templates directory, as follows:

   ```
   $ mkdir templates && cd templates && touch upload-file.html
   ```

2. Copy the following content to upload-file.html:

   ```html
   <html>
     <head>
       <meta charset="utf-8">
       <title>File Upload</title>
     </head>
     <body>
       <form action="/upload" method="post" enctype="multipart/
       form-data">
         <label for="file">File:</label>
         <input type="file" name="file" id="file">
         <input type="submit" name="submit" value="Submit">
       </form>
     </body>
   </html>
   ```

   In the preceding template, we defined a field of type file along with a Submit button.

   On clicking the **Submit** button, the client encodes the data that forms the body of the request and makes a POST call to the form action, which is /upload in our case.

3. Create upload-file.go, where we will define handlers to render the file upload template, get the file from the request, process it, and write the response to an HTTP response stream, as follows:

   ```go
   package main
   import
   (
     "fmt"
     "html/template"
     "io"
     "log"
     "net/http"
   ```

```go
    "os"
)
const
(
  CONN_HOST = "localhost"
  CONN_PORT = "8080"
)
func fileHandler(w http.ResponseWriter, r *http.Request)
{
  file, header, err := r.FormFile("file")
  if err != nil
  {
    log.Printf("error getting a file for the provided form key : ",
    err)
    return
  }
  defer file.Close()
  out, pathError := os.Create("/tmp/uploadedFile")
  if pathError != nil
  {
    log.Printf("error creating a file for writing : ", pathError)
    return
  }
  defer out.Close()
  _, copyFileError := io.Copy(out, file)
  if copyFileError != nil
  {
    log.Printf("error occurred while file copy : ", copyFileError)
  }
  fmt.Fprintf(w, "File uploaded successfully : "+header.Filename)
}
func index(w http.ResponseWriter, r *http.Request)
{
  parsedTemplate, _ := template.ParseFiles("templates/
  upload-file.html")
  parsedTemplate.Execute(w, nil)
}
func main()
{
  http.HandleFunc("/", index)
  http.HandleFunc("/upload", fileHandler)
  err := http.ListenAndServe(CONN_HOST+":"+CONN_PORT, nil)
  if err != nil
  {
    log.Fatal("error starting http server : ", err)
    return
  }
}
```

With everything in place, the directory structure should look like the following:

4. Run the program with the following command:

```
$ go run upload-file.go
```

How it works...

Once we run the program, the HTTP server will start locally listening on port `8080`. Browsing `http://localhost:8080` will show us the File Upload Form, as shown in the following screenshot:

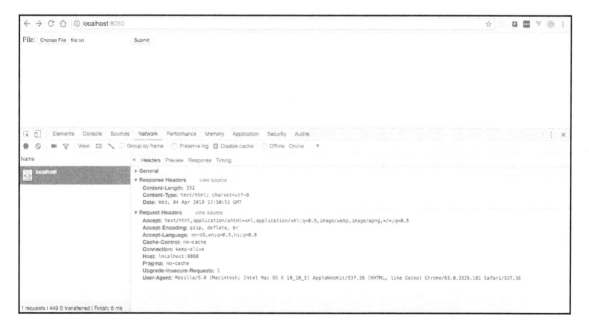

Pressing the **Submit** button after choosing a file will result in the creation of a file on the server with the name as `uploadedFile` inside the `/tmp` directory. You can see this by executing the following commands:

```
→    ~  cd ~ && cd /tmp && ls -l
total 0
-rw-r--r--   1 ArpitAggarwal   wheel   0 Apr   4 23:24 uploadedFile
→    /tmp
```

Also, the successful upload will display the message on the browser, as shown in the following screenshot:

Let's understand the Go program we have written:

We defined the `fileHandler()` handler, which gets the file from the request, reads its content, and eventually writes it onto a file on a server. As this handler does a lot of things, let's go through it in detail:

- `file, header, err := r.FormFile("file")`: Here we call the `FormFile` handler on the HTTP request to get the file for the provided form key.
- `if err != nil { log.Printf("error getting a file for the provided form key : ", err) return }`: Here we check whether there is any problem while getting the file from the request. If there is, then log the error and exit with a status code of `1`.
- `defer file.Close()`: The `defer` statement closes the `file` once we return from the function.
- `out, pathError := os.Create("/tmp/uploadedFile")`: Here we are creating a file named `uploadedFile` inside a `/tmp` directory with mode `666`, which means the client can read and write but cannot execute the file.
- `if pathError != nil { log.Printf("error creating a file for writing : ", pathError) return }`: Here we check whether there are any problems with creating a file on the server. If there are, then log the error and exit with a status code of `1`.
- `_, copyFileError := io.Copy(out, file)`: Here we copy content from the file we received to the file we created inside the `/tmp` directory.
- `fmt.Fprintf(w, "File uploaded successfully : "+header.Filename)`: Here we write a message along with a filename to an HTTP response stream.

Working with Sessions, Error Handling, and Caching in Go

3

In this chapter, we will cover the following recipes:

- Creating your first HTTP session
- Managing your HTTP session using Redis
- Creating your first HTTP cookie
- Implementing caching in Go
- Implementing HTTP error handling in Go
- Implementing login and logout in a web application

Introduction

Sometimes, we would like to persist information such as user data at an application level rather than persisting it in a database, which can be easily achieved using sessions and cookies. The difference between the two is that sessions are stored on the server side, whereas cookies are stored on the client side. We may also need to cache static data to avoid unnecessary calls to a database or a web service, and implement error handling while developing a web application. With knowledge of the concepts covered in this chapter, we will be able to implement all these functionalities in a fairly easy way.

In this chapter, we will start with creating an HTTP session, then we will learn how we can manage it using Redis, creating cookies, caching HTTP responses, implementing error handling, and eventually end with implementing login and logout mechanisms in Go.

Creating your first HTTP session

HTTP is a stateless protocol, which means each time a client retrieves a web page, the client opens a separate connection to the server and the server responds to it without keeping any record of the previous client request. So, if we want to implement a mechanism where the server knows about a request that the client has sent to it, then we can implement it using a session.

When we are working with sessions, clients just need to send an ID and the data is loaded from the server for the corresponding ID. There are three ways that we can implement this in a web application:

- Cookies
- Hidden form fields
- URL rewriting

In this recipe, we will implement a session using HTTP cookies.

How to do it...

1. Install the `github.com/gorilla/sessions` package using the `go get` command, as follows:

   ```
   $ go get github.com/gorilla/sessions
   ```

2. Create `http-session.go` where we will create a Gorilla cookie store to save and retrieve session information defining three handlers—`/login`, `/home`, and `/logout`—where we will be creating a valid session cookie, writing a response to an HTTP response stream, and invalidating a session cookie respectively, as follows:

   ```
   package main
   import
   (
     "fmt"
     "log"
     "net/http"
     "github.com/gorilla/sessions"
   )
   const
   (
     CONN_HOST = "localhost"
   ```

```go
    CONN_PORT = "8080"
)
var store *sessions.CookieStore
func init()
{
  store = sessions.NewCookieStore([]byte("secret-key"))
}
func home(w http.ResponseWriter, r *http.Request)
{
  session, _ := store.Get(r, "session-name")
  var authenticated interface{} = session.Values["authenticated"]
  if authenticated != nil
  {
    isAuthenticated := session.Values["authenticated"].(bool)
    if !isAuthenticated
    {
      http.Error(w, "You are unauthorized to view the page",
      http.StatusForbidden)
      return
    }
    fmt.Fprintln(w, "Home Page")
  }
  else
  {
    http.Error(w, "You are unauthorized to view the page",
    http.StatusForbidden)
    return
  }
}
func login(w http.ResponseWriter, r *http.Request)
{
  session, _ := store.Get(r, "session-name")
  session.Values["authenticated"] = true
  session.Save(r, w)
  fmt.Fprintln(w, "You have successfully logged in.")
}
func logout(w http.ResponseWriter, r *http.Request)
{
  session, _ := store.Get(r, "session-name")
  session.Values["authenticated"] = false
  session.Save(r, w)
  fmt.Fprintln(w, "You have successfully logged out.")
}
func main()
{
  http.HandleFunc("/home", home)
  http.HandleFunc("/login", login)
  http.HandleFunc("/logout", logout)
```

```
err := http.ListenAndServe(CONN_HOST+":"+CONN_PORT, nil)
if err != nil
{
  log.Fatal("error starting http server : ", err)
  return
}
}
```

3. Run the program with the following command:

```
$ go run http-session.go
```

How it works...

Once we run the program, the HTTP server will start listening locally on port 8080.

Next, we will execute a couple of commands to see how the session works.

First, we will access /home by executing the following command:

```
$ curl -X GET http://localhost:8080/home
```

This will result in an unauthorized access message from the server as shown in the following screenshot:

```
~ ~ curl -X GET http://localhost:8080/home
You are unauthorized to view the page
```

This is because we first have to log in to an application, which will create a session ID that the server will validate before providing access to any web page. So, let's log in to the application:

```
$ curl -X GET -i http://localhost:8080/login
```

Executing the previous command will give us the `Cookie`, which has to be set as a request header to access any web page:

```
    $ curl -X GET -i http://localhost:8080/login
HTTP/1.1 200 OK
Set-Cookie: session-name=MTUyMzEwMTI3NXxEdi1CQkFFQ180SUFBUkFCRUFBQUpmLUNBQUVHYzNSeWFXNW5EQThBRFdGMWRHaGxibGJwWTJGMFpXUUVZbTl2YVkFJQ0FBRT18ou7Zxn3qSbqHHiajubn23Eiv8a348AhPlBRN3uTRM4M=
; Path=/; Expires=Mon, 07 May 2018 11:41:15 GMT; Max-Age=2592000
Date: Sat, 07 Apr 2018 11:41:15 GMT
Content-Length: 33
Content-Type: text/plain; charset=utf-8

You have successfully logged in.
```

Next, we will use this provided `Cookie` to access `/home`, as follows:

```
$ curl --cookie "session-
name=MTUyMzEwMTI3NXxEdi1CQkFFQ180SUFBUkFCRUFBQUpmLUNBQUVHYzNSeWFXNW5EQThBRF
dGMWRHaGxiblJwWTJGMFpXUUVZbTl2YkFJQ0FBRT18ou7Zxn3qSbqHHiajubn23Eiv8a348AhPl
8RN3uTRM4M=;" http://localhost:8080/home
```

This results in the home page as a response from the server:

```
    $ curl --cookie "session-name=MTUyMzEwMTI3NXxEdi1CQkFFQ180SUFBUkFCRUFBQUpmLUNBQUVHYzNSeWFXNW5EQThBRFdGMWRHaGxiblJwWTJGMFpXUUVZbTl2YkFJQ0FBRT18ou7Zxn3qSbqHHiajubn23Eiv8a348AhPlBRN
3uTRM4M=;" http://localhost:8080/home
Home Page
```

Let's understand the Go program we have written:

- Using `var store *sessions.CookieStore`, we declared a private cookie store to store sessions using secure cookies.
- Using `func init() { store = sessions.NewCookieStore([]byte("secret-key")) }`, we defined an `init()` function that runs before `main()` to create a new cookie store and assign it to the `store`.

 `init()` is always called, regardless of whether there's a main function or not, so if you import a package that has an `init` function, it will be executed.

- Next, we defined a `home` handler where we get a session from the cookie store for the given name after adding it to the registry using `store.Get` and fetch the value of the `authenticated` key from the cache. If it is true, then we write `Home Page` to an HTTP response stream; otherwise, we write a **You are unauthorized to view the page.** message along with a `403` HTTP code.

- Next, we defined a `login` handler where we again get a session, set the `authenticated` key with a value of `true`, save it, and finally write **You have successfully logged in.** to an HTTP response stream.
- Next, we defined a `logout` handler where we get a session, set an `authenticated` key with the value of `false`, save it, and finally write **You have successfully logged out.** to an HTTP response stream.
- Finally, we defined `main()` where we mapped all handlers, `home`, `login`, and `logout`, to `/home`, `/login`, and `/logout` respectively, and start the HTTP server on `localhost:8080`.

Managing your HTTP session using Redis

While working with the distributed applications, we probably have to implement stateless load balancing for frontend users. This is so we can persist session information in a database or a filesystem so that we can identify the user and retrieve their information if a server gets shut down or restarted.

We will be solving this problem as part of the recipe using Redis as the persistent store to save a session.

Getting ready…

As we have already created a session variable in our previous recipe using the Gorilla cookie store, we will just extend this recipe to save session information in Redis rather than maintaining it on the server.

There are multiple implementations of the Gorilla session store, which you can find at `https://github.com/gorilla/sessions#store-implementations`. As we are using Redis as our backend store, we will be using `https://github.com/boj/redistore`, which depends on the Redigo Redis library to store a session.

This recipe assumes you have Redis and Redis Browser installed and running locally on ports `6379` and `4567` respectively.

How to do it...

1. Install `gopkg.in/boj/redistore.v1` and `github.com/gorilla/sessions` using the `go get` command, as follows:

   ```
   $ go get gopkg.in/boj/redistore.v1
   $ go get github.com/gorilla/sessions
   ```

2. Create `http-session-redis.go`, where we will create a `RedisStore` to store and retrieve session variables, as follows:

   ```go
   package main
   import
   (
     "fmt"
     "log"
     "net/http"
     "github.com/gorilla/sessions"
     redisStore "gopkg.in/boj/redistore.v1"
   )
   const
   (
     CONN_HOST = "localhost"
     CONN_PORT = "8080"
   )
   var store *redisStore.RediStore
   var err error
   func init()
   {
     store, err = redisStore.NewRediStore(10, "tcp", ":6379", "",
     []byte("secret-key"))
     if err != nil
     {
       log.Fatal("error getting redis store : ", err)
     }
   }
   func home(w http.ResponseWriter, r *http.Request)
   {
     session, _ := store.Get(r, "session-name")
     var authenticated interface{} = session.Values["authenticated"]
     if authenticated != nil
     {
       isAuthenticated := session.Values["authenticated"].(bool)
       if !isAuthenticated
       {
         http.Error(w, "You are unauthorized to view the page",
   ```

```go
        http.StatusForbidden)
        return
      }
      fmt.Fprintln(w, "Home Page")
    }
    else
    {
      http.Error(w, "You are unauthorized to view the page",
      http.StatusForbidden)
      return
    }
}
func login(w http.ResponseWriter, r *http.Request)
{
  session, _ := store.Get(r, "session-name")
  session.Values["authenticated"] = true
  if err = sessions.Save(r, w); err != nil
  {
    log.Fatalf("Error saving session: %v", err)
  }
  fmt.Fprintln(w, "You have successfully logged in.")
}
func logout(w http.ResponseWriter, r *http.Request)
{
  session, _ := store.Get(r, "session-name")
  session.Values["authenticated"] = false
  session.Save(r, w)
  fmt.Fprintln(w, "You have successfully logged out.")
}
func main()
{
  http.HandleFunc("/home", home)
  http.HandleFunc("/login", login)
  http.HandleFunc("/logout", logout)
  err := http.ListenAndServe(CONN_HOST+":"+CONN_PORT, nil)
  defer store.Close()
  if err != nil
  {
    log.Fatal("error starting http server : ", err)
    return
  }
}
```

3. Run the program with the following command:

```
$ go run http-session-redis.go
```

How it works...

Once we run the program, the HTTP server will start locally listening on port 8080.

Next, we will execute a couple of commands to see how the session works.

First, we will access /home by executing the following command:

```
$ curl -X GET http://localhost:8080/home
```

This will result in an unauthorized access message from the server as shown in the following screenshot:

```
→   ~ curl -X GET http://localhost:8080/home
You are unauthorized to view the page
```

This is because we first have to log in to an application, which will create a **session ID** that the server will validate before providing access to any web page. So, let's log in to the application:

```
$ curl -X GET -i http://localhost:8080/login
```

Executing the previous command will give us the Cookie, which has to be set as a request header to access any web page:

```
→   ~ curl -X GET -i http://localhost:8080/login
HTTP/1.1 200 OK
Set-Cookie: session-name=MTUyMzEwNDUyM3xOd3dBTkv4T1JrdzNURFkyUkVWWlQxWklUekpKVUVOWE1saFRUMHBHVTB4T1RGVXlSRU5RVkZWWk5VeFNWVmRPVVZSQk4wTk1RMUU9fAlGgLGU-OHxoP78xzEHMoiuY0Q4rrbsXfajSS6H
iJAm; Path=/; Expires=Mon, 07 May 2018 12:35:23 GMT; Max-Age=2592000
Date: Sat, 07 Apr 2018 12:35:23 GMT
Content-Length: 33
Content-Type: text/plain; charset=utf-8

You have successfully logged in.
```

Once the previous command is executed, a `Cookie` will be created and saved in Redis, which you can see by executing the command from `redis-cli` or in the **Redis Browser**, as shown in the following screenshot:

Next, we will use the `Cookie` provided to access `/home`, as follows:

```
$ curl --cookie "session-
name=MTUyMzEwNDUyM3xOd3dBTkV4T1JrdzNURFkyUkVWWlQxWklUekpKVUVOWE1saFRUMHBHVT
B4T1RGVXlSRU5RVkZWWk5VeFNWVmRPVVZSQk4wTk1RMUU9fAlGgLGU-
OHxoP78xzEHMoiuY0Q4rrbsXfajSS6HiJAm;" http://localhost:8080/home
```

This results in the Home Page as a response from the server:

```
.. curl --cookie "session-name=MTUyMzEwNDUyM3xOd3dBTkV4T1JrdzNURFkyUkVWWlQxWklUekpKVUVOWE1saFRUMHBHVTB4T1RGVXlSRU5RVkZWWk5VeFNWVmRPVVZSQk4wTk1RMUU9fAlGgLGU-OHxoP78xzEHMoiuY0Q4rrbs
XfajSS6HiJAm;" http://localhost:8080/home
Home Page
```

Let's understand the changes we introduced in this recipe:

1. Using `var store *redisStore.RediStore`, we declared a private `RediStore` to store sessions in Redis.
2. Next, we updated the `init()` function to create `NewRediStore` with a size and maximum number of idle connections as `10`, and assigned it to the store. If there is an error while creating a store, then we log the error and exit with a status code of `1`.
3. Finally, we updated `main()` to introduce the `defer store.Close()` statement, which closes the Redis store once we return from the function.

Creating your first HTTP cookie

Cookies play an important role when storing information on the client side and we can use their values to identify a user. Basically, cookies were invented to solve the problem of remembering information about the user or persistent-login authentication, which refers to websites being able to remember the identity of a principal between sessions.

Cookies are simple text files that web browsers create when you visit websites on the internet. Your device stores the text files locally, allowing your browser to access the cookie and pass data back to the original website, and are saved in name-value pairs.

How to do it...

1. Install the `github.com/gorilla/securecookie` package using the `go get` command, as follows:

```
$ go get github.com/gorilla/securecookie
```

2. Create `http-cookie.go`, where we will create a Gorilla secure cookie to store and retrieve cookies, as follows:

```
package main
import
(
  "fmt"
  "log"
  "net/http"
  "github.com/gorilla/securecookie"
)
const
(
  CONN_HOST = "localhost"
  CONN_PORT = "8080"
)
var cookieHandler *securecookie.SecureCookie
func init()
{
  cookieHandler = securecookie.New(securecookie.
  GenerateRandomKey(64),
  securecookie.GenerateRandomKey(32))
}
func createCookie(w http.ResponseWriter, r *http.Request)
{
  value := map[string]string
```

```go
  {
    "username": "Foo",
  }
  base64Encoded, err := cookieHandler.Encode("key", value)
  if err == nil
  {
    cookie := &http.Cookie
    {
      Name: "first-cookie",
      Value: base64Encoded,
      Path: "/",
    }
    http.SetCookie(w, cookie)
  }
  w.Write([]byte(fmt.Sprintf("Cookie created.")))
}
func readCookie(w http.ResponseWriter, r *http.Request)
{
  log.Printf("Reading Cookie..")
  cookie, err := r.Cookie("first-cookie")
  if cookie != nil && err == nil
  {
    value := make(map[string]string)
    if err = cookieHandler.Decode("key", cookie.Value, &value);
    err == nil
    {
      w.Write([]byte(fmt.Sprintf("Hello %v \n",
      value["username"])))
    }
  }
  else
  {
    log.Printf("Cookie not found..")
    w.Write([]byte(fmt.Sprint("Hello")))
  }
}

func main()
{
  http.HandleFunc("/create", createCookie)
  http.HandleFunc("/read", readCookie)
  err := http.ListenAndServe(CONN_HOST+":"+CONN_PORT, nil)
  if err != nil
  {
    log.Fatal("error starting http server : ", err)
    return
  }
}
```

3. Run the program with the following command:

```
$ go run http-cookie.go
```

How it works...

Once we run the program, the HTTP server will start locally listening on port 8080.

Browsing `http://localhost:8080/read` will display **Hello** in the browser, as you can see in the following screenshot:

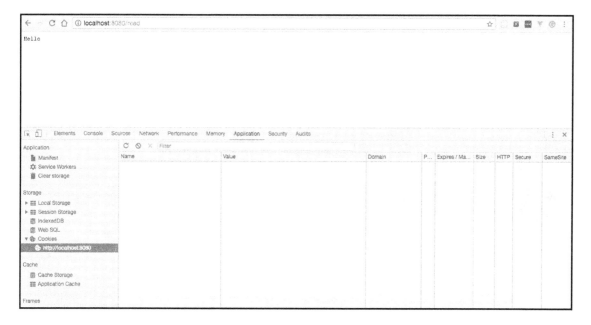

Next, we will access `http://localhost:8080/create`, which will create a cookie with the name **first-cookie** and display the Cookie created message in the browser:

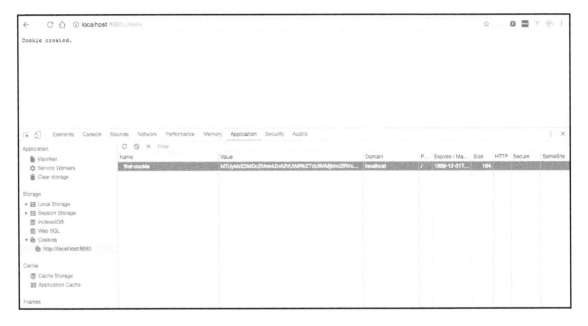

Now, subsequent access to `http://localhost:8080/read` will use **first-cookie** to display **Hello**, followed by the value of first-cookie, as follows:

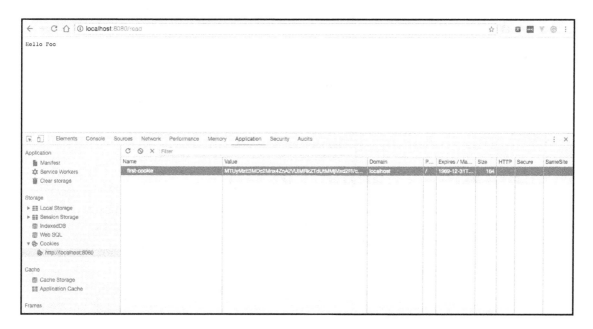

Let's understand the program we have written:

- Using `import ("fmt" "log" "net/http" "github.com/gorilla/securecookie")`, we introduced an additional package—`github.com/gorilla/securecookie`, which we will use to encode and decode authenticated and encrypted cookie values.
- Using `var cookieHandler *securecookie.SecureCookie`, we declared a private secure cookie.
- Next, we updated the `init()` function to create `SecureCookie` passing a 64-byte hash key, which is used to authenticate values using HMAC and a 32-byte block key, which is used to encrypt values.
- Next, we defined a `createCookie` handler where we create a `Base64` encoded cookie with the key as `username` and the value as `Foo` using an `Encode` handler of `gorilla/securecookie`. Then, we add a `Set-Cookie` header to the provided `ResponseWriter` headers and write a `Cookie created.` message to an HTTP response.

- Next, we defined a `readCookie` handler, where we retrieve a cookie from the request, which is `first-cookie` in our code, get a value for it, and write it to an HTTP response.
- Finally, we defined `main()` where we mapped all handlers—`createCookie` and `readCookie`—to `/create` and `/read` respectively, and started the HTTP server on `localhost:8080`.

Implementing caching in Go

Caching data in a web application is sometimes necessary to avoid requesting static data from a database or external service again and again. Go does not provide any built-in package to cache responses, but it does support it through external packages.

There are a number of packages, such as `https://github.com/coocood/freecache` and `https://github.com/patrickmn/go-cache`, which can help in implementing caching and, in this recipe, we will be using the `https://github.com/patrickmn/go-cache` to implement it.

How to do it…

1. Install the `github.com/patrickmn/go-cache` package using the `go get` command, as follows:

   ```
   $ go get github.com/patrickmn/go-cache
   ```

2. Create `http-caching.go`, where we will create a cache and populate it with data on server boot up, as follows:

   ```
   package main
   import
   (
     "fmt"
     "log"
     "net/http"
     "time"
     "github.com/patrickmn/go-cache"
   )
   const
   (
     CONN_HOST = "localhost"
   ```

```
    CONN_PORT = "8080"
)
var newCache *cache.Cache
func init()
{
  newCache = cache.New(5*time.Minute, 10*time.Minute)
  newCache.Set("foo", "bar", cache.DefaultExpiration)
}
func getFromCache(w http.ResponseWriter, r *http.Request)
{
  foo, found := newCache.Get("foo")
  if found
  {
    log.Print("Key Found in Cache with value as :: ",
    foo.(string))
    fmt.Fprintf(w, "Hello "+foo.(string))
  }
  else
  {
    log.Print("Key Not Found in Cache :: ", "foo")
    fmt.Fprintf(w, "Key Not Found in Cache")
  }
}
func main()
{
  http.HandleFunc("/", getFromCache)
  err := http.ListenAndServe(CONN_HOST+":"+CONN_PORT, nil)
  if err != nil
  {
    log.Fatal("error starting http server : ", err)
    return
  }
}
```

3. Run the program with the following command:

```
$ go run http-caching.go
```

How it works...

Once we run the program, the HTTP server will start locally listening on port `8080`.

On startup, the key with the name `foo` with a value as `bar` will be added to the cache.

Browsing `http://localhost:8080/` will read a key value from the cache and append it to **Hello** as shown in the following screenshot:

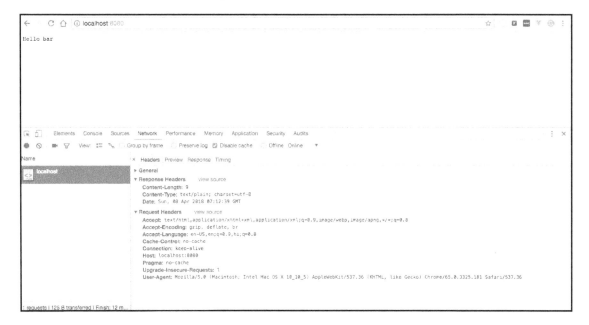

We have specified the cache data expiration time in our program as five minutes, which means the key that we have created in the cache at server startup will not be there after five minutes. So, accessing the same URL again after five minutes will return **Key Not Found in the Cache** from the server, as follows:

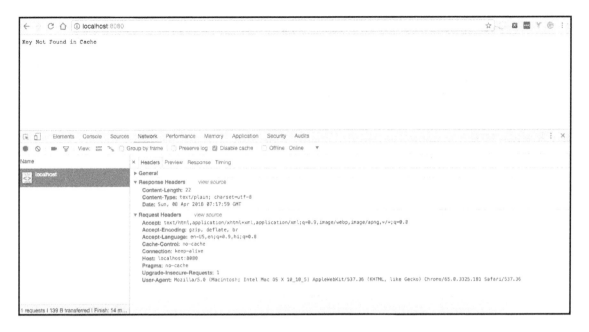

Let's understand the program we have written:

1. Using `var newCache *cache.Cache`, we declared a private cache.
2. Next, we updated the `init()` function where we create a cache with five minutes of expiration time and 10 minutes of cleanup interval, and add an item to the cache with a key as `foo` with its value as `bar` and its expiration value as `0`, which means we want to use the cache's default expiration time.

> If the expiration duration is less than one (or `NoExpiration`), the items in the cache never expire (by default) and must be deleted manually. If the cleanup interval is less than one, expired items are not deleted from the cache before calling `c.DeleteExpired()`.

3. Next, we defined the `getFromCache` handler where we retrieve the value for a key from the cache. If found, we write it to an HTTP response; otherwise, we write the `Key Not Found in Cache` message to an HTTP response.

Implementing HTTP error handling in Go

Implementing error handling in any web application is one of the main aspects because it helps in troubleshooting and fixing bugs faster. Error handling means whenever an error occurs in an application, it should be logged somewhere, either in a file or in a database with the proper error message, along with the stack trace.

In Go, it can be implemented in multiple ways. One way is to write custom handlers, which we will be covering in this recipe.

How to do it...

1. Install the `github.com/gorilla/mux` package using the `go get` command, as follows:

   ```
   $ go get github.com/gorilla/mux
   ```

2. Create `http-error-handling.go`, where we will create a custom handler that acts as a wrapper to handle all the HTTP requests, as follows:

   ```go
   package main
   import
   (
     "errors"
     "fmt"
     "log"
     "net/http"
     "strings"
     "github.com/gorilla/mux"
   )
   const
   (
     CONN_HOST = "localhost"
     CONN_PORT = "8080"
   )
   type NameNotFoundError struct
   {
     Code int
     Err error
   }
   func (nameNotFoundError NameNotFoundError) Error() string
   {
     return nameNotFoundError.Err.Error()
   }
   ```

```
type WrapperHandler func(http.ResponseWriter, *http.Request)
error
func (wrapperHandler WrapperHandler) ServeHTTP(w http.
ResponseWriter, r *http.Request)
{
  err := wrapperHandler(w, r)
  if err != nil
  {
    switch e := err.(type)
    {
      case NameNotFoundError:
      log.Printf("HTTP %s - %d", e.Err, e.Code)
      http.Error(w, e.Err.Error(), e.Code)
      default:
      http.Error(w, http.StatusText(http.
      StatusInternalServerError),
      http.StatusInternalServerError)
    }
  }
}
func getName(w http.ResponseWriter, r *http.Request) error
{
  vars := mux.Vars(r)
  name := vars["name"]
  if strings.EqualFold(name, "foo")
  {
    fmt.Fprintf(w, "Hello "+name)
    return nil
  }
  else
  {
    return NameNotFoundError{500, errors.New("Name Not Found")}
  }
}
func main()
{
  router := mux.NewRouter()
  router.Handle("/employee/get/{name}",
  WrapperHandler(getName)).Methods("GET")
  err := http.ListenAndServe(CONN_HOST+":"+CONN_PORT, router)
  if err != nil
  {
    log.Fatal("error starting http server : ", err)
    return
  }
}
```

3. Run the program with the following command:

```
$ go run http-error-handling.go
```

How it works...

Once we run the program, the HTTP server will start locally listening on port 8080.

Next, browsing `http://localhost:8080/employee/get/foo` will give us the **Hello**, followed by the employee name with the status code as 200, as a response in the browser:

On the other hand, accessing `http://localhost:8080/employee/get/bar` will return us an HTTP error with the message **Name Not Found** and an error code of 500:

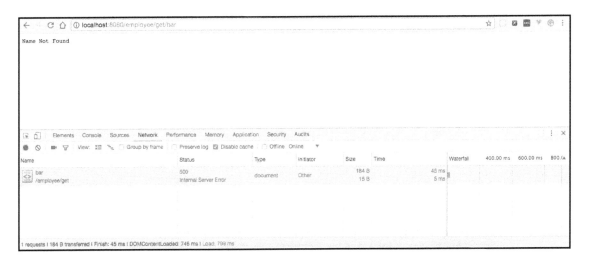

Let's understand the program we have written:

1. We defined a `NameNotFoundError` struct with two fields—`Code` of type `int` and `Err` of type `error`, which represents an error with an associated HTTP status code, as follows:

```
type NameNotFoundError struct
{
  Code int
  Err error
}
```

2. Then, we allowed `NameNotFoundError` to satisfy the error interface, as follows:

```
func (nameNotFoundError NameNotFoundError) Error() string
{
  return nameNotFoundError.Err.Error()
}
```

3. Next, we defined a user-defined type `WrapperHandler`, which is a Go function that accepts any handler that accepts `func(http.ResponseWriter, *http.Request)` as input parameters and returns an error.

4. Then, we defined a `ServeHTTP` handler, which calls a handler we pass to `WrapperHandler` passing `(http.ResponseWriter, *http.Request)` as parameters to it and checks if there are any errors returned by the handler. If there are, then it handles them appropriately using the switch case, as follows:

```
if err != nil
{
  switch e := err.(type)
  {
    case NameNotFoundError:
    log.Printf("HTTP %s - %d", e.Err, e.Code)
    http.Error(w, e.Err.Error(), e.Code)
    default:
    http.Error(w, http.StatusText(http.
    StatusInternalServerError),
    http.StatusInternalServerError)
  }
}
```

5. Next, we defined a `getName` handler, which extracts request path variables, gets the value of the `name` variable, and checks if the name matches `foo`. If so, then it writes **Hello**, followed by the name, to an HTTP response; otherwise, it returns a `NameNotFoundError` struct with a `Code` field value of `500` and an `err` field value of an `error` with the text `Name Not Found`.

6. Finally, we defined `main()`, where we registered `WrapperHandler` as a handler to be called for the URL pattern as `/get/{name}`.

Implementing login and logout in web application

Whenever we want an application to be accessed by registered users, we have to implement a mechanism that asks for the user's credentials before allowing them to view any web pages, which we will be covering in this recipe.

Getting ready...

As we have already created an HTML form in one of our previous recipes, we will just update it to implement login and logout mechanisms using the `gorilla/securecookie` package.

 See the *Implementing login and logout in web application* recipe in `Chapter 2`, *Working with Templates, Static Files, and HTML Forms.*

How to do it...

1. Install `github.com/gorilla/mux` and `github.com/gorilla/securecookie` using the `go get` command, as follows:

   ```
   $ go get github.com/gorilla/mux
   $ go get github.com/gorilla/securecookie
   ```

2. Create `home.html` inside the `templates` directory, as follows:

   ```
   $ mkdir templates && cd templates && touch home.html
   ```

3. Copy the following content to `home.html`:

   ```html
   <html>
     <head>
       <title></title>
     </head>
     <body>
       <h1>Welcome {{.userName}}!</h1>
       <form method="post" action="/logout">
         <button type="submit">Logout</button>
       </form>
     </body>
   </html>
   ```

   In the preceding template, we defined a placeholder, `{{.userName}}`, whose values will be substituted by the template engine at runtime and a **Logout** button. By clicking the **Logout** button, the client will make a POST call to a form action, which is `/logout` in our case.

4. Create `html-form-login-logout.go`, where we will parse the login form, read the username field, and set a session cookie when a user clicks the **Login** button. We also clear the session once a user clicks the **Logout** button, as follows:

```go
package main
import
(
  "html/template"
  "log"
  "net/http"
  "github.com/gorilla/mux"
  "github.com/gorilla/securecookie"
)
const
(
  CONN_HOST = "localhost"
  CONN_PORT = "8080"
)
var cookieHandler = securecookie.New
(
  securecookie.GenerateRandomKey(64),
  securecookie.GenerateRandomKey(32)
)
func getUserName(request *http.Request) (userName string)
{
  cookie, err := request.Cookie("session")
  if err == nil
  {
    cookieValue := make(map[string]string)
    err = cookieHandler.Decode("session", cookie.Value,
    &cookieValue)
    if err == nil
    {
      userName = cookieValue["username"]
    }
  }
  return userName
}
func setSession(userName string, response http.ResponseWriter)
{
  value := map[string]string
  {
    "username": userName,
  }
  encoded, err := cookieHandler.Encode("session", value)
  if err == nil
  {
```

```
    cookie := &http.Cookie
    {
      Name: "session",
      Value: encoded,
      Path: "/",
    }
    http.SetCookie(response, cookie)
  }
}
func clearSession(response http.ResponseWriter)
{
  cookie := &http.Cookie
  {
    Name: "session",
    Value: "",
    Path: "/",
    MaxAge: -1,
  }
  http.SetCookie(response, cookie)
}
func login(response http.ResponseWriter, request *http.Request)
{
  username := request.FormValue("username")
  password := request.FormValue("password")
  target := "/"
  if username != "" && password != ""
  {
    setSession(username, response)
    target = "/home"
  }
  http.Redirect(response, request, target, 302)
}
func logout(response http.ResponseWriter, request *http.Request)
{
  clearSession(response)
  http.Redirect(response, request, "/", 302)
}
func loginPage(w http.ResponseWriter, r *http.Request)
{
  parsedTemplate, _ := template.ParseFiles("templates/
  login-form.html")
  parsedTemplate.Execute(w, nil)
}
func homePage(response http.ResponseWriter, request *http.Request)
{
  userName := getUserName(request)
  if userName != ""
  {
```

```go
      data := map[string]interface{}
      {
        "userName": userName,
      }
      parsedTemplate, _ := template.ParseFiles("templates/home.html")
      parsedTemplate.Execute(response, data)
    }
    else
    {
      http.Redirect(response, request, "/", 302)
    }
}
func main()
{
  var router = mux.NewRouter()
  router.HandleFunc("/", loginPage)
  router.HandleFunc("/home", homePage)
  router.HandleFunc("/login", login).Methods("POST")
  router.HandleFunc("/logout", logout).Methods("POST")
  http.Handle("/", router)
  err := http.ListenAndServe(CONN_HOST+":"+CONN_PORT, nil)
  if err != nil
  {
    log.Fatal("error starting http server : ", err)
    return
  }
}
```

With everything in place, the directory structure should look like the following:

5. Run the program with the following command:

```
$ go run html-form-login-logout.go
```

How it works...

Once we run the program, the HTTP server will start listening locally on port `8080`.

Next, browsing `http://localhost:8080` will show us the login form, as shown in the following screenshot:

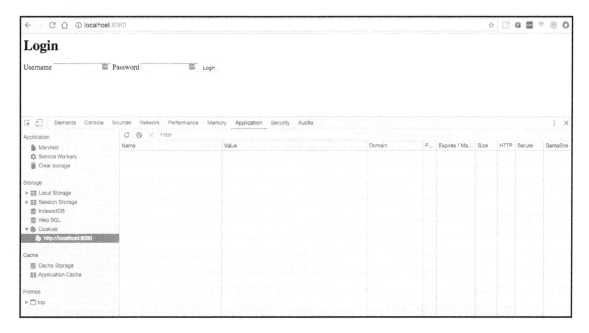

Submitting the form after entering the username `Foo` and a random password will render the **Welcome Foo!** message in the browser and create a cookie with the name **session**, which manages the user login/logout state:

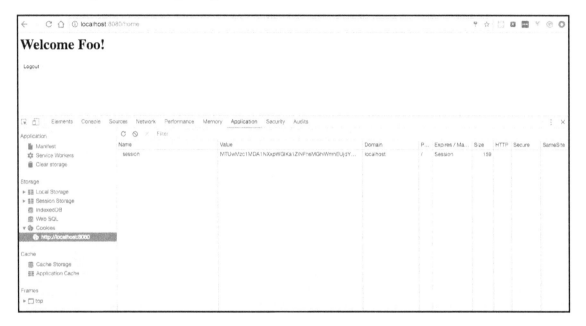

Now, every subsequent request to `http://localhost:8080/home` will display the **Welcome Foo!** message in the browser until the cookie with the name **session** exists.

Next, accessing `http://localhost:8080/home` after clearing the cookie will redirect us to `http://localhost:8080/` and show us the login form:

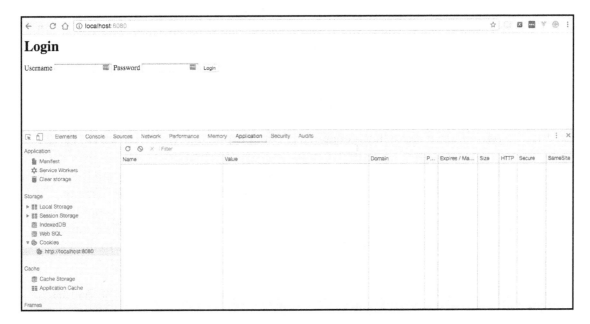

Let's understand the program we have written.

1. Using `var cookieHandler = securecookie.New(securecookie.GenerateRandomKey(64), securecookie.GenerateRandomKey(32))`, we are creating a secure cookie, passing a hash key as the first argument, and a block key as the second argument. The hash key is used to authenticate values using HMAC and the block key is used to encrypt values.

2. Next, we defined a `getUserName` handler, where we get a cookie from the HTTP request, initialize a `cookieValue` map of string `keys` to string `values`, decode a cookie, and get a value for the username and return.

3. Next, we defined a `setSession` handler, where we create and initialize a map with the `key` and `value` as `username`, serialize it, sign it with a message authentication code, encode it using a `cookieHandler.Encode` handler, create a new HTTP cookie, and write it to an HTTP response stream.

4. Next, we defined `clearSession`, which basically sets the value of the cookie as empty and writes it to an HTTP response stream.

5. Next, we defined a `login` handler, where we get a username and password from an HTTP form, check if both are not empty, then call a `setSession` handler and redirect to `/home`, otherwise, redirect to the root URL `/`.

6. Next, we defined a `logout` handler, where we clear the session values calling the `clearSession` handler and redirect to the root URL.

7. Next, we defined a `loginPage` handler, where we parse `login-form.html`, return a new template with the name and its content, call the `Execute` handler on a parsed template, which generates HTML output, and write it to an HTTP response stream.

8. Next, we defined a `homePage` handler, which gets the username from the HTTP request calling the `getUserName` handler. Then, we check whether it is not empty or whether there is a cookie value present. If the username is not blank, we parse `home.html`, inject the username as a data map, generate HTML output, and write it to an HTTP response stream; otherwise, we redirect it to the root URL `/`.

Finally, we defined the `main()` method, where we start the program execution. As this method does a lot of things, let's look at it line by line:

- `var router = mux.NewRouter()`: Here, we create a new router instance.
- `router.HandleFunc("/", loginPage)`: Here, we are registering the `loginPageHandler` handler with the `/` URL pattern using `HandleFunc` of the `gorilla/mux` package, which means the `loginPage` handler gets executed by passing `(http.ResponseWriter, *http.Request)` as parameters to it whenever we access the HTTP URL with the `/` pattern.
- `router.HandleFunc("/home", homePage)`: Here, we are registering the `homePageHandler` handler with the `/home` URL pattern using the `HandleFunc` of the `gorilla/mux` package, which means the `homePage` handler gets executed by passing `(http.ResponseWriter, *http.Request)` as parameters to it whenever we access the HTTP URL with the `/home` pattern.

- `router.HandleFunc("/login", login).Methods("POST")`: Here, we are registering the `loginHandler` handler with the `/login` URL pattern using the `HandleFunc` of the `gorilla/mux` package, which means the `login` handler gets executed by passing (`http.ResponseWriter`, `*http.Request`) as parameters to it whenever we access the HTTP URL with the `/login` pattern.

- `router.HandleFunc("/logout", logout).Methods("POST")`: Here, we are registering the `logoutHandler` handler with the `/logout` URL pattern using the `HandleFunc` of the `gorilla/mux` package, which means the `logout` handler gets executed by passing (`http.ResponseWriter`, `*http.Request`) as parameters to it whenever we access the HTTP URL with the `/logout` pattern.

- `http.Handle("/", router)`: Here, we are registering the router for the `/` URL pattern using `HandleFunc` of the `net/http` package, which means all requests with the `/` URL pattern are handled by the router handler.

- `err := http.ListenAndServe(CONN_HOST+":"+CONN_PORT, nil)`: Here, we are calling `http.ListenAndServe` to serve HTTP requests that handle each incoming connection in a separate Goroutine. `ListenAndServe` accepts two parameters—server address and handler, where the server address is `localhost:8080` and the handler is `nil`, which means we are asking the server to use `DefaultServeMux` as a handler.

- `if err != nil { log.Fatal("error starting http server : ", err) return}`: Here, we check if there are any problems with starting the server. If there are, then log the error and exit with a status code of 1.

4
Writing and Consuming RESTful Web Services in Go

In this chapter, we will cover the following recipes:

- Creating your first HTTP GET method
- Creating your first HTTP POST method
- Creating your first HTTP PUT method
- Creating your first HTTP DELETE method
- Versioning your REST API
- Creating your first REST client
- Creating your first AngularJS client
- Creating your first ReactJS client
- Creating your first VueJS client

Introduction

Whenever we build a web application that encapsulates logic that could be helpful to other related applications, we will often also write and consume web services. This is because they expose functionality over a network, which is accessible through the HTTP protocol, making an application a single source of truth.

In this chapter, we will write a RESTful API that supports GET, POST, PUT, and DELETE HTTP methods, and then we will learn how we can version the REST API, which is very helpful when we are creating APIs consumed publicly. We will finish up with writing the REST client to consume them.

Creating your first HTTP GET method

While writing web applications, we often have to expose our services to the client or to the UI so that they can consume a piece of code running on a different system. Exposing the service can be done with HTTP protocol methods. Out of the many HTTP methods, we will be learning to implement the HTTP GET method in this recipe.

How to do it...

1. Install the `github.com/gorilla/mux` package using the `go get` command, as follows:

   ```
   $ go get github.com/gorilla/mux
   ```

2. Create `http-rest-get.go` where we will define two routes—`/employees` and `/employee/{id}` along with their handlers. The former writes the static array of employees and the latter writes employee details for the provided ID to an HTTP response stream, as follows:

   ```go
   package main
   import
   (
     "encoding/json"
     "log"
     "net/http"
     "github.com/gorilla/mux"
   )
   const
   (
     CONN_HOST = "localhost"
     CONN_PORT = "8080"
   )
   type Route struct
   {
     Name string
     Method string
     Pattern string
     HandlerFunc http.HandlerFunc
   }
   type Routes []Route
   var routes = Routes
   {
     Route
   ```

```
        {
          "getEmployees",
          "GET",
          "/employees",
          getEmployees,
        },
        Route
        {
          "getEmployee",
          "GET",
          "/employee/{id}",
          getEmployee,
        },
}
type Employee struct
{
    Id string `json:"id"`
    FirstName string `json:"firstName"`
    LastName string `json:"lastName"`
}
type Employees []Employee
var employees []Employee
func init()
{
    employees = Employees
    {
        Employee{Id: "1", FirstName: "Foo", LastName: "Bar"},
        Employee{Id: "2", FirstName: "Baz", LastName: "Qux"},
    }
}
func getEmployees(w http.ResponseWriter, r *http.Request)
{
    json.NewEncoder(w).Encode(employees)
}
func getEmployee(w http.ResponseWriter, r *http.Request)
{
    vars := mux.Vars(r)
    id := vars["id"]
    for _, employee := range employees
    {
        if employee.Id == id
        {
            if err := json.NewEncoder(w).Encode(employee); err != nil
            {
                log.Print("error getting requested employee :: ", err)
            }
        }
    }
```

```go
}
func AddRoutes(router *mux.Router) *mux.Router
{
  for _, route := range routes
  {
    router.
    Methods(route.Method).
    Path(route.Pattern).
    Name(route.Name).
    Handler(route.HandlerFunc)
  }
  return router
}
func main()
{
  muxRouter := mux.NewRouter().StrictSlash(true)
  router := AddRoutes(muxRouter)
  err := http.ListenAndServe(CONN_HOST+":"+CONN_PORT, router)
  if err != nil
  {
    log.Fatal("error starting http server :: ", err)
    return
  }
}
```

3. Run the program with the following command:

```
$ go run http-rest-get.go
```

How it works...

Once we run the program, the HTTP server will start locally listening on port 8080.

Next, executing a GET request from the command line as follows will give you a list of all the employees:

```
$ curl -X GET http://localhost:8080/employees
[{"id":"1","firstName":"Foo","lastName":"Bar"},{"id":"2","firstName":"Baz",
"lastName":"Qux"}]
```

Here, executing a GET request for a particular employee ID from the command line as follows, will give you the employee details for the corresponding ID:

```
$ curl -X GET http://localhost:8080/employee/1
{"id":"1","firstName":"Foo","lastName":"Bar"}
```

Let's understand the program we have written:

1. We used import ("encoding/json" "log" "net/http" "strconv" "github.com/gorilla/mux"). Here, we imported github.com/gorilla/mux to create a Gorilla Mux Router.

2. Next, we declared the Route struct type with four fields—Name, Method, Pattern, and HandlerFunc, where Name represents the name of an HTTP method, Method represents the HTTP method type which can be GET, POST, PUT, DELETE, and so on, Pattern represents the URL path, and HandlerFunc represents the HTTP handler.

3. Next, we defined two routes for the GET request, as follows:

```
var routes = Routes
{
  Route
  {
    "getEmployees",
    "GET",
    "/employees",
    getEmployees,
  },
  Route
  {
    "getEmployee",
    "GET",
    "/employee/{id}",
    getEmployee,
  },
}
```

4. Next, we defined a static `Employees` array, as follows:

```
func init()
{
  employees = Employees
  {
    Employee{Id: "1", FirstName: "Foo", LastName: "Bar"},
    Employee{Id: "2", FirstName: "Baz", LastName: "Qux"},
  }
}
```

5. Then, we defined two handlers—`getEmployees` and `getEmployee` where the former just marshals a static array of employees and writes it to an HTTP response stream, and the latter gets the employee ID from an HTTP request variable, fetches the employee for the corresponding ID from the array, marshals the object, and writes it to an HTTP response stream.

6. Following the handlers, we defined an `AddRoutes` function, which iterates over the routes array we defined, adds it to the `gorilla/mux` router, and returns the `Router` object.

7. Finally, we defined `main()` where we create a `gorilla/mux` router instance using the `NewRouter()` handler with the trailing slash behavior for new routes as true, which means the application will always see the path as specified in the route. For example, if the route path is `/path/`, accessing `/path` will redirect to the former and vice versa.

Creating your first HTTP POST method

Whenever we have to send data to the server either through an asynchronous call or through an HTML form, then we go with the HTTP `POST` method implementation, which we will cover in this recipe.

How to do it...

1. Install the `github.com/gorilla/mux` package using the `go get` command, as follows:

```
$ go get github.com/gorilla/mux
```

2. Create `http-rest-post.go` where we will define an additional route that supports the HTTP `POST` method and a handler that adds an employee to the initial static array of employees and writes the updated list to an HTTP response stream, as follows:

```go
package main
import
(
  "encoding/json"
  "log"
  "net/http"
  "github.com/gorilla/mux"
)
const
(
  CONN_HOST = "localhost"
  CONN_PORT = "8080"
)
type Route struct
{
  Name string
  Method string
  Pattern string
  HandlerFunc http.HandlerFunc
}
type Routes []Route
var routes = Routes
{
  Route
  {
    "getEmployees",
    "GET",
    "/employees",
    getEmployees,
  },
  Route
  {
    "addEmployee",
    "POST",
    "/employee/add",
    addEmployee,
  },
}
type Employee struct
{
  Id string `json:"id"`
  FirstName string `json:"firstName"`
```

```go
    LastName string `json:"lastName"`
}
type Employees []Employee
var employees []Employee
func init()
{
  employees = Employees
  {
    Employee{Id: "1", FirstName: "Foo", LastName: "Bar"},
    Employee{Id: "2", FirstName: "Baz", LastName: "Qux"},
  }
}
func getEmployees(w http.ResponseWriter, r *http.Request)
{
  json.NewEncoder(w).Encode(employees)
}
func addEmployee(w http.ResponseWriter, r *http.Request)
{
  employee := Employee{}
  err := json.NewDecoder(r.Body).Decode(&employee)
  if err != nil
  {
    log.Print("error occurred while decoding employee
    data :: ", err)
    return
  }
  log.Printf("adding employee id :: %s with firstName
  as :: %s and lastName as :: %s ", employee.Id,
  employee.FirstName, employee.LastName)
  employees = append(employees, Employee{Id: employee.Id,
  FirstName: employee.FirstName, LastName: employee.LastName})
  json.NewEncoder(w).Encode(employees)
}
func AddRoutes(router *mux.Router) *mux.Router
{
  for _, route := range routes
  {
    router.
    Methods(route.Method).
    Path(route.Pattern).
    Name(route.Name).
    Handler(route.HandlerFunc)
  }
  return router
}
func main()
{
  muxRouter := mux.NewRouter().StrictSlash(true)
```

```
router := AddRoutes(muxRouter)
err := http.ListenAndServe(CONN_HOST+":"+CONN_PORT, router)
if err != nil
{
  log.Fatal("error starting http server :: ", err)
  return
}
}
```

3. Run the program with the following command:

```
$ go run http-rest-post.go
```

How it works...

Once we run the program, the HTTP server will start locally listening on port 8080.

Next, executing a POST request from the command line as follows will add an employee to the list with ID as 3 and return the list of employees as a response:

```
$ curl -H "Content-Type: application/json" -X POST -d '{"Id":"3",
"firstName":"Quux", "lastName":"Corge"}' http://localhost:8080/employee/add
```

This is shown in the following screenshot:

```
 curl -H "Content-Type: application/json" -X POST -d '{"Id":"3", "firstName":"Quux", "lastName":"Corge"}' http://localhost:8080/employee/add
[{"id":"1","firstName":"Foo","lastName":"Bar"},{"id":"2","firstName":"Baz","lastName":"Qux"},{"id":"3","firstName":"Quux","lastName":"Corge"}]
```

Let's understand the change we introduced in this recipe:

1. First, we added another route with the name addEmployee that executes the addEmployee handler for every POST request for the URL pattern /employee/add.

2. Then, we defined an addEmployee handler, which basically decodes the employee data that comes as part of a POST request using the NewDecoder handler of the built-in encoding/json package of Go, appends it to the initial static array of an employee, and writes it to an HTTP response stream.

Creating your first HTTP PUT method

Whenever we want to update a record that we have created earlier or want to create a new record if it does not exist, often termed an **Upsert,** then we go with the HTTP PUT method implementation, which we will cover in this recipe.

How to do it...

1. Install the `github.com/gorilla/mux` package using the `go get` command, as follows:

   ```
   $ go get github.com/gorilla/mux
   ```

2. Create `http-rest-put.go` where we will define an additional route that supports the HTTP PUT method and a handler that either updates the employee details for the provided ID or adds an employee to the initial static array of employees; if the ID does not exist, marshal it to the JSON, and write it to an HTTP response stream, as follows:

   ```
   package main
   import
   (
     "encoding/json"
     "log"
     "net/http"
     "github.com/gorilla/mux"
   )
   const
   (
     CONN_HOST = "localhost"
     CONN_PORT = "8080"
   )
   type Route struct
   {
     Name string
     Method string
     Pattern string
     HandlerFunc http.HandlerFunc
   }
   type Routes []Route
   var routes = Routes
   {
     Route
   ```

```go
        {
          "getEmployees",
          "GET",
          "/employees",
          getEmployees,
        },
        Route
        {
          "addEmployee",
          "POST",
          "/employee/add",
          addEmployee,
        },
        Route
        {
          "updateEmployee",
          "PUT",
          "/employee/update",
          updateEmployee,
        },
}
type Employee struct
{
  Id string `json:"id"`
  FirstName string `json:"firstName"`
  LastName string `json:"lastName"`
}
type Employees []Employee
var employees []Employee
func init()
{
  employees = Employees
  {
    Employee{Id: "1", FirstName: "Foo", LastName: "Bar"},
    Employee{Id: "2", FirstName: "Baz", LastName: "Qux"},
  }
}
func getEmployees(w http.ResponseWriter, r *http.Request)
{
  json.NewEncoder(w).Encode(employees)
}
func updateEmployee(w http.ResponseWriter, r *http.Request)
{
  employee := Employee{}
  err := json.NewDecoder(r.Body).Decode(&employee)
  if err != nil
  {
    log.Print("error occurred while decoding employee
```

```go
    data :: ", err)
    return
  }
  var isUpsert = true
  for idx, emp := range employees
  {
    if emp.Id == employee.Id
    {
      isUpsert = false
      log.Printf("updating employee id :: %s with
      firstName as :: %s and lastName as:: %s ",
      employee.Id, employee.FirstName, employee.LastName)
      employees[idx].FirstName = employee.FirstName
      employees[idx].LastName = employee.LastName
      break
    }
  }
  if isUpsert
  {
    log.Printf("upserting employee id :: %s with
    firstName as :: %s and lastName as:: %s ",
    employee.Id, employee.FirstName, employee.LastName)
    employees = append(employees, Employee{Id: employee.Id,
    FirstName: employee.FirstName, LastName: employee.LastName})
  }
  json.NewEncoder(w).Encode(employees)
}
func addEmployee(w http.ResponseWriter, r *http.Request)
{
  employee := Employee{}
  err := json.NewDecoder(r.Body).Decode(&employee)
  if err != nil
  {
    log.Print("error occurred while decoding employee
    data :: ", err)
    return
  }
  log.Printf("adding employee id :: %s with firstName
  as :: %s and lastName as :: %s ", employee.Id,
  employee.FirstName, employee.LastName)
  employees = append(employees, Employee{Id: employee.Id,
  FirstName: employee.FirstName, LastName: employee.LastName})
  json.NewEncoder(w).Encode(employees)
}
func AddRoutes(router *mux.Router) *mux.Router
{
  for _, route := range routes
  {
```

```
      router.
      Methods(route.Method).
      Path(route.Pattern).
      Name(route.Name).
      Handler(route.HandlerFunc)
    }
    return router
  }
  func main()
  {
    muxRouter := mux.NewRouter().StrictSlash(true)
    router := AddRoutes(muxRouter)
    err := http.ListenAndServe(CONN_HOST+":"+CONN_PORT, router)
    if err != nil
    {
      log.Fatal("error starting http server :: ", err)
      return
    }
  }
```

3. Run the program with the following command:

```
$ go run http-rest-put.go
```

How it works...

Once we run the program, the HTTP server will start locally listening on port 8080.

Next, executing a PUT request from the command line as follows, will update the firstName and the lastName for an employee with ID 1:

```
$ curl -H "Content-Type: application/json" -X PUT -d '{"Id":"1",
"firstName":"Grault", "lastName":"Garply"}'
http://localhost:8080/employee/update
```

This can be seen in the following screenshot:

```
  curl -H "Content-Type: application/json" -X PUT -d '{"Id":"1", "firstName":"Grault", "lastName":"Garply"}' http://localhost:8080/employee/update
[{"id":"1","firstName":"Grault","lastName":"Garply"},{"id":"2","firstName":"Baz","lastName":"Qux"}]
```

If we execute a PUT request for an employee with ID 3 from the command line as follows, it will add another employee to the array, as there is no employee with ID 3, demonstrating the upsert scenario:

```
$ curl -H "Content-Type: application/json" -X PUT -d '{"Id":"3",
"firstName":"Quux", "lastName":"Corge"}'
http://localhost:8080/employee/update
```

This can be seen in the following screenshot:

```
curl -H "Content-Type: application/json" -X PUT -d '{"Id":"3", "firstName":"Quux", "lastName":"Corge"}' http://localhost:8080/employee/update
[{"id":"1","firstName":"Grault","lastName":"Garply"},{"id":"2","firstName":"Baz","lastName":"Qux"},{"id":"3","firstName":"Quux","lastName":"Corge"}]
```

Let's understand the change we introduced in this recipe:

1. First, we added another route with the name updateEmployee, which executes the updateEmployee handler for every PUT request for the URL pattern /employee/update.

2. Then, we defined an updateEmployee handler, which basically decodes the employee data that comes as part of a PUT request using the NewDecoder handler of the built-in encoding/json package of Go, iterates over the employees array to know whether the employee ID requested exists in the initial static array of employees, which we may also term as an UPDATE or UPSERT scenario, performs the required action, and writes the response to an HTTP response stream.

Creating your first HTTP DELETE method

Whenever we want to remove a record that is no longer required then we go with the HTTP DELETE method implementation, which we will cover in this recipe.

How to do it...

1. Install the github.com/gorilla/mux package, using the go get command, as follows:

```
$ go get github.com/gorilla/mux
```

2. Create `http-rest-delete.go` where we will define a route that supports the HTTP `DELETE` method and a handler that deletes the employee details for the provided ID from the static array of employees, marshals the array to JSON, and writes it to an HTTP response stream, as follows:

```go
package main
import
(
  "encoding/json"
  "log"
  "net/http"
  "github.com/gorilla/mux"
)
const
(
  CONN_HOST = "localhost"
  CONN_PORT = "8080"
)
type Route struct
{
  Name string
  Method string
  Pattern string
  HandlerFunc http.HandlerFunc
}
type Routes []Route
var routes = Routes
{
  Route
  {
    "getEmployees",
    "GET",
    "/employees",
    getEmployees,
  },
  Route
  {
    "addEmployee",
    "POST",
    "/employee/add/",
    addEmployee,
  },
  Route
  {
    "deleteEmployee",
    "DELETE",
    "/employee/delete",
```

```
      deleteEmployee,
    },
  }
type Employee struct
{
  Id string `json:"id"`
  FirstName string `json:"firstName"`
  LastName string `json:"lastName"`
}
type Employees []Employee
var employees []Employee
func init()
{
  employees = Employees
  {
    Employee{Id: "1", FirstName: "Foo", LastName: "Bar"},
    Employee{Id: "2", FirstName: "Baz", LastName: "Qux"},
  }
}
func getEmployees(w http.ResponseWriter, r *http.Request)
{
  json.NewEncoder(w).Encode(employees)
}
func deleteEmployee(w http.ResponseWriter, r *http.Request)
{
  employee := Employee{}
  err := json.NewDecoder(r.Body).Decode(&employee)
  if err != nil
  {
    log.Print("error occurred while decoding employee
    data :: ", err)
    return
  }
  log.Printf("deleting employee id :: %s with firstName
  as :: %s and lastName as :: %s ", employee.Id,
  employee.FirstName, employee.LastName)
  index := GetIndex(employee.Id)
  employees = append(employees[:index], employees[index+1:]...)
  json.NewEncoder(w).Encode(employees)
}
func GetIndex(id string) int
{
  for i := 0; i < len(employees); i++
  {
    if employees[i].Id == id
    {
      return i
    }
```

```go
  }
  return -1
}
func addEmployee(w http.ResponseWriter, r *http.Request)
{
  employee := Employee{}
  err := json.NewDecoder(r.Body).Decode(&employee)
  if err != nil
  {
    log.Print("error occurred while decoding employee
    data :: ", err)
    return
  }
  log.Printf("adding employee id :: %s with firstName
  as :: %s and lastName as :: %s ", employee.Id,
  employee.FirstName, employee.LastName)
  employees = append(employees, Employee{Id: employee.Id,
  FirstName: employee.FirstName, LastName: employee.LastName})
  json.NewEncoder(w).Encode(employees)
}
func AddRoutes(router *mux.Router) *mux.Router
{
  for _, route := range routes
  {
    router.
    Methods(route.Method).
    Path(route.Pattern).
    Name(route.Name).
    Handler(route.HandlerFunc)
  }
  return router
}
func main()
{
  muxRouter := mux.NewRouter().StrictSlash(true)
  router := AddRoutes(muxRouter)
  err := http.ListenAndServe(CONN_HOST+":"+CONN_PORT, router)
  if err != nil
  {
    log.Fatal("error starting http server :: ", err)
    return
  }
}
```

3. Run the program with the following command:

```
$ go run http-rest-delete.go
```

How it works...

Once we run the program, the HTTP server will start locally listening on port 8080.

Next, executing a DELETE request from the command line as follows, will delete an employee with ID 1 and give us the updated list of employees:

```
$ curl -H "Content-Type: application/json" -X DELETE -d '{"Id":"1",
"firstName": "Foo", "lastName": "Bar"}'
http://localhost:8080/employee/delete
```

This can be seen in the following screenshot:

```
    curl -H "Content-Type: application/json" -X DELETE -d '{"Id":"1", "firstName": "Foo", "lastName": "Bar"}' http://localhost:8080/employee/delete
[{"id":"2","firstName":"Baz","lastName":"Qux"}]
```

Let's understand the change we introduced in this recipe:

1. First, we added another route with the name deleteEmployee, which executes the deleteEmployee handler for every DELETE request for the URL pattern /employee/delete.

2. Then, we defined a deleteEmployee handler, which basically decodes the employee data that comes as part of a DELETE request using the NewDecoder handler of the built-in encoding/json package of Go, gets the index of the requested employee using the GetIndex helper function, deletes the employee, and writes the updated array as JSON to an HTTP response stream.

Versioning your REST API

When you create a RESTful API to serve an internal client, you probably don't have to worry about versioning your API. Taking things a step further, if you have control over all the clients that access your API, the same may be true.

However, in a case where you have a public API or an API where you do not have control over every client using it, versioning of your API may be required, as businesses need to evolve, which we will be covering in this recipe.

How to do it...

1. Install the `github.com/gorilla/mux` package, using the `go get` command, as follows:

   $ go get github.com/gorilla/mux

2. Create `http-rest-versioning.go` where we will define two versions of the same URL path that support the HTTP `GET` method, with one having `v1` as a prefix and the other one with `v2` as a prefix in the route, as follows:

```go
package main
import
(
   "encoding/json"
   "log"
   "net/http"
   "strings"
   "github.com/gorilla/mux"
)
const
(
   CONN_HOST = "localhost"
   CONN_PORT = "8080"
)
type Route struct
{
   Name string
   Method string
   Pattern string
   HandlerFunc http.HandlerFunc
}
type Routes []Route
var routes = Routes
{
   Route
   {
      "getEmployees",
      "GET",
      "/employees",
      getEmployees,
   },
}
type Employee struct
{
   Id string `json:"id"`
```

```go
    FirstName string `json:"firstName"`
    LastName string `json:"lastName"`
}
type Employees []Employee
var employees []Employee
var employeesV1 []Employee
var employeesV2 []Employee
func init()
{
  employees = Employees
  {
    Employee{Id: "1", FirstName: "Foo", LastName: "Bar"},
  }
  employeesV1 = Employees
  {
    Employee{Id: "1", FirstName: "Foo", LastName: "Bar"},
    Employee{Id: "2", FirstName: "Baz", LastName: "Qux"},
  }
  employeesV2 = Employees
  {
    Employee{Id: "1", FirstName: "Baz", LastName: "Qux"},
    Employee{Id: "2", FirstName: "Quux", LastName: "Quuz"},
  }
}
func getEmployees(w http.ResponseWriter, r *http.Request)
{
  if strings.HasPrefix(r.URL.Path, "/v1")
  {
    json.NewEncoder(w).Encode(employeesV1)
  }
  else if strings.HasPrefix(r.URL.Path, "/v2")
  {
    json.NewEncoder(w).Encode(employeesV2)
  }
  else
  {
    json.NewEncoder(w).Encode(employees)
  }
}
func AddRoutes(router *mux.Router) *mux.Router
{
  for _, route := range routes
  {
    router.
    Methods(route.Method).
    Path(route.Pattern).
    Name(route.Name).
    Handler(route.HandlerFunc)
```

```
    }
    return router
}
func main()
{
    muxRouter := mux.NewRouter().StrictSlash(true)
    router := AddRoutes(muxRouter)
    // v1
    AddRoutes(muxRouter.PathPrefix("/v1").Subrouter())
    // v2
    AddRoutes(muxRouter.PathPrefix("/v2").Subrouter())
    err := http.ListenAndServe(CONN_HOST+":"+CONN_PORT, router)
    if err != nil
    {
        log.Fatal("error starting http server :: ", err)
        return
    }
}
```

3. Run the program with the following command:

```
$ go run http-rest-versioning.go
```

How it works...

Once we run the program, the HTTP server will start locally listening on port 8080.

Next, executing a GET request with the path prefix as /v1 from the command line as follows, will give you a list of one set of employees:

```
$ curl -X GET http://localhost:8080/v1/employees
[{"id":"1","firstName":"Foo","lastName":"Bar"},{"id":"2","firstName":"Baz",
"lastName":"Qux"}]
```

Here, executing a GET request with path prefix as /v2 will give you a list of another set of employees, as follows:

```
$ curl -X GET http://localhost:8080/v2/employees
[{"id":"1","firstName":"Baz","lastName":"Qux"},{"id":"2","firstName":"Quux"
,"lastName":"Quuz"}]
```

Sometimes, while designing the REST URL, we prefer to return the default data if the client queries the endpoint without specifying the version in the URL path. To incorporate it, we have modified the `getEmployees` handler to check for the prefix in the URL and act accordingly. So, executing a `GET` request without the path prefix from the command line as follows, will give you a list with a single record, which we can call the default or initial response of the REST endpoint called:

```
$ curl -X GET http://localhost:8080/employees
[{"id":"1","firstName":"Foo","lastName":"Bar"}]
```

Let's understand the change we introduced in this recipe:

1. First, we defined a single route with the name `getEmployees`, which executes a `getEmployees` handler for every `GET` request for the URL pattern `/employees`.
2. Then, we created three arrays, namely `employees`, `employeesV1`, and `employeesV2`, which are returned as a response to an HTTP `GET` call for the URL patterns `/employees`, `/v1/employees`, and `/v2/employees` respectively.
3. Next, we have defined a `getEmployees` handler where we check for the prefix in the URL path and perform an action based on it.
4. Then, we defined an `AddRoutes` helper function, which iterates over the routes array we defined, adds it to the `gorilla/mux` router, and returns the `Router` object.
5. Finally, we defined `main()` where we create a `gorilla/mux` router instance using the `NewRouter()` handler with the trailing slash behavior for new routes as true, and add routes to it calling the `AddRoutes` helper function passing the default router and two subrouters, one with the prefix as `v1` and the other with the prefix as `v2`.

Creating your first REST client

Today, most applications that communicate with servers use RESTful services. Based on our needs, we consume these services through JavaScript, jQuery, or through a REST client.

In this recipe, we will write a REST client using the `https://gopkg.in/resty.v1` package, which itself is inspired by the Ruby rest client to consume the RESTful services.

Getting ready...

Run `http-rest-get.go`, which we created in one of our previous recipes, in a separate terminal, executing the following command:

```
$ go run http-rest-get.go
```

 See the *Creating your first HTTP GET method* recipe.

Verify whether the `/employees` service is running locally on port `8080` by executing the following command:

```
$ curl -X GET http://localhost:8080/employees
```

This should return the following response:

```
[{"id":"1","firstName":"Foo","lastName":"Bar"},{"id":"2","firstName":"Baz",
"lastName":"Qux"}]
```

How to do it...

1. Install the `github.com/gorilla/mux` and `gopkg.in/resty.v1` packages using the `go get` command, as follows:

```
$ go get github.com/gorilla/mux
$ go get -u gopkg.in/resty.v1
```

2. Create `http-rest-client.go` where we will define handlers that call `resty` handlers, such as `GET`, `POST`, `PUT`, and `DELETE`, get the response from the REST service, and write it to an HTTP response stream, as follows:

```
package main
import
(
  "encoding/json"
  "fmt"
  "log"
  "net/http"
  "github.com/gorilla/mux"
  resty "gopkg.in/resty.v1"
)
```

```go
const
(
  CONN_HOST = "localhost"
  CONN_PORT = "8090"
)
const WEB_SERVICE_HOST string = "http://localhost:8080"
type Employee struct
{
  Id string `json:"id"`
  FirstName string `json:"firstName"`
  LastName string `json:"lastName"`
}
func getEmployees(w http.ResponseWriter, r *http.Request)
{
  response, err := resty.R().Get(WEB_SERVICE_HOST +
  "/employees")
  if err != nil
  {
    log.Print("error getting data from the web service :: ", err)
    return
  }
  printOutput(response, err)
  fmt.Fprintf(w, response.String())
}
func addEmployee(w http.ResponseWriter, r *http.Request)
{
  employee := Employee{}
  decodingErr := json.NewDecoder(r.Body).Decode(&employee)
  if decodingErr != nil
  {
    log.Print("error occurred while decoding employee
    data :: ", decodingErr)
    return
  }
  log.Printf("adding employee id :: %s with firstName
  as :: %s and lastName as :: %s ", employee.Id,
  employee.FirstName, employee.LastName)
  response, err := resty.R().
  SetHeader("Content-Type", "application/json").
  SetBody(Employee{Id: employee.Id, FirstName:
  employee.FirstName, LastName: employee.LastName}).
  Post(WEB_SERVICE_HOST + "/employee/add")
  if err != nil
  {
    log.Print("error occurred while adding employee :: ", err)
    return
  }
  printOutput(response, err)
```

```
    fmt.Fprintf(w, response.String())
}
func updateEmployee(w http.ResponseWriter, r *http.Request)
{
  employee := Employee{}
  decodingErr := json.NewDecoder(r.Body).Decode(&employee)
  if decodingErr != nil
  {
    log.Print("error occurred while decoding employee
    data :: ", decodingErr)
    return
  }
  log.Printf("updating employee id :: %s with firstName
  as :: %s and lastName as :: %s ", employee.Id,
  employee.FirstName, employee.LastName)
  response, err := resty.R().
  SetBody(Employee{Id: employee.Id, FirstName:
  employee.FirstName, LastName: employee.LastName}).
  Put(WEB_SERVICE_HOST + "/employee/update")
  if err != nil
  {
    log.Print("error occurred while updating employee :: ", err)
    return
  }
  printOutput(response, err)
  fmt.Fprintf(w, response.String())
}
func deleteEmployee(w http.ResponseWriter, r *http.Request)
{
  employee := Employee{}
  decodingErr := json.NewDecoder(r.Body).Decode(&employee)
  if decodingErr != nil
  {
    log.Print("error occurred while decoding employee
    data :: ", decodingErr)
    return
  }
  log.Printf("deleting employee id :: %s with firstName
  as :: %s and lastName as :: %s ", employee.Id,
  employee.FirstName, employee.LastName)
  response, err := resty.R().
  SetBody(Employee{Id: employee.Id, FirstName:
  employee.FirstName, LastName: employee.LastName}).
  Delete(WEB_SERVICE_HOST + "/employee/delete")
  if err != nil
  {
    log.Print("error occurred while deleting employee :: ", err)
    return
```

```
    }
    printOutput(response, err)
    fmt.Fprintf(w, response.String())
}
func printOutput(resp *resty.Response, err error)
{
    log.Println(resp, err)
}
func main()
{
    router := mux.NewRouter().StrictSlash(false)
    router.HandleFunc("/employees", getEmployees).Methods("GET")
    employee := router.PathPrefix("/employee").Subrouter()
    employee.HandleFunc("/add", addEmployee).Methods("POST")
    employee.HandleFunc("/update", updateEmployee).Methods("PUT")
    employee.HandleFunc("/delete", deleteEmployee).Methods("DELETE")
    err := http.ListenAndServe(CONN_HOST+":"+CONN_PORT, router)
    if err != nil
    {
        log.Fatal("error starting http server : ", err)
        return
    }
}
```

3. Run the program with the following command:

```
$ go run http-rest-client.go
```

How it works...

Once we run the program, the HTTP server will start locally listening on port 8090.

Next, executing a GET request to the REST client from the command line as follows will give you a list of all the employees from the service:

```
$ curl -X GET http://localhost:8090/employees
[{"id":"1","firstName":"Foo","lastName":"Bar"},{"id":"2","firstName":"Baz",
"lastName":"Qux"}]
```

Similarly, run http-rest-post.go, which we created in one of our previous recipes, in a separate terminal by executing the following command:

```
$ go run http-rest-post.go
```

Execute a POST request to the REST client from the command line, as follows:

```
$ curl -H "Content-Type: application/json" -X POST -d '{"Id":"3",
"firstName":"Quux", "lastName":"Corge"}' http://localhost:8090/employee/add
[{"id":"1","firstName":"Foo","lastName":"Bar"},{"id":"2","firstName":"Baz",
"lastName":"Qux"},{"id":"3","firstName":"Quux","lastName":"Corge"}]
```

This will add an employee to the initial static list and return an updated list of the employees, which will look as shown in the following screenshot:

```
~ curl -H "Content-Type: application/json" -X POST -d '{"Id":"3", "firstName":"Quux", "lastName":"Corge"}' http://localhost:8090/employee/add
[{"id":"1","firstName":"Foo","lastName":"Bar"},{"id":"2","firstName":"Baz","lastName":"Qux"},{"id":"3","firstName":"Quux","lastName":"Corge"}]
```

Let's understand the program we have written:

1. Using import ("encoding/json" "fmt" "log" "net/http" "github.com/gorilla/mux" resty "gopkg.in/resty.v1"), we imported github.com/gorilla/mux to create a Gorilla Mux Router and gopkg.in/resty.v1 with the package alias as resty, which is a REST client of Go, having various handlers to consume the RESTful web service.

2. Using const WEB_SERVICE_HOST string = "http://localhost:8080", we declared the complete URL of the RESTful web service host.

> Depending on the project size, you can move the WEB_SERVICE_HOST string to the constants file or to the properties file, helping you to override its value at runtime.

3. Next, we defined a getEmployees handler where we create a new resty request object calling its R() handler, call the Get method, which performs the HTTP GET request, gets the response, and writes it to an HTTP response.

4. Similarly, we defined three more handlers that do the POST, PUT, and DELETE requests to the RESTful service and a main() where we create a gorilla/mux router instance and register the /employees URL path with the getEmployees handler and /employee/add, /employee/update, and /employee/delete with the addEmployee, updateEmployee, and deleteEmployee handlers, respectively.

Creating your first AngularJS Client

AngularJS is an open source JavaScript Model-View-Whatever (MVW) framework, which lets us build well-structured, easily testable and maintainable browser-based applications.

In this recipe, we will learn to create an AngularJS with TypeScript 2 client to send a POST request to the HTTP server running locally.

Getting ready...

As we have already created an HTTP server that accepts both GET and POST requests in one of our previous recipes, we will be using the same code base as our HTTP server.

Also, this recipe assumes you have Angular2 CLI installed on your machine. If not, install it by executing the following command:

```
$ npm install -g @angular/cli
```

See the *Creating your first HTTP POST method* recipe.

How to do it...

1. Create a new project and skeleton application by executing the following command:

   ```
   $ ng new angularjs-client
   ```

2. Move to the angularjs-client directory and create server.go by executing the following command:

   ```
   $ cd angularjs-client && touch server.go
   ```

3. Copy the following code to `server.go`:

```go
package main
import
(
  "encoding/json"
  "log"
  "net/http"
  "github.com/gorilla/mux"
)
const
(
  CONN_HOST = "localhost"
  CONN_PORT = "8080"
)
type Route struct
{
  Name string
  Method string
  Pattern string
  HandlerFunc http.HandlerFunc
}
type Routes []Route
var routes = Routes
{
  Route
  {
    "getEmployees",
    "GET",
    "/employees",
    getEmployees,
  },
  Route
  {
    "addEmployee",
    "POST",
    "/employee/add",
    addEmployee,
  },
}
type Employee struct
{
  Id string `json:"id"`
  FirstName string `json:"firstName"`
  LastName string `json:"lastName"`
}
type Employees []Employee
```

```go
var employees []Employee
func init()
{
  employees = Employees
  {
    Employee{Id: "1", FirstName: "Foo", LastName: "Bar"},
    Employee{Id: "2", FirstName: "Baz", LastName: "Qux"},
  }
}
func getEmployees(w http.ResponseWriter, r *http.Request)
{
  json.NewEncoder(w).Encode(employees)
}
func addEmployee(w http.ResponseWriter, r *http.Request)
{
  employee := Employee{}
  err := json.NewDecoder(r.Body).Decode(&employee)
  if err != nil
  {
    log.Print("error occurred while decoding employee
    data :: ", err)
    return
  }
  log.Printf("adding employee id :: %s with firstName
  as :: %s and lastName as :: %s ", employee.Id,
  employee.FirstName, employee.LastName)
  employees = append(employees, Employee{Id: employee.Id,
  FirstName: employee.FirstName, LastName: employee.LastName})
  json.NewEncoder(w).Encode(employees)
}
func AddRoutes(router *mux.Router) *mux.Router
{
  for _, route := range routes
  {
    router.
    Methods(route.Method).
    Path(route.Pattern).
    Name(route.Name).
    Handler(route.HandlerFunc)
  }
  return router
}
func main()
{
  muxRouter := mux.NewRouter().StrictSlash(true)
  router := AddRoutes(muxRouter)
  router.PathPrefix("/").Handler(http.FileServer
  (http.Dir("./dist/")))
```

```
    err := http.ListenAndServe(CONN_HOST+":"+CONN_PORT, router)
    if err != nil
    {
      log.Fatal("error starting http server :: ", err)
      return
    }
}
```

4. Move to the `angularjs-client` directory and create `models/employee.ts` and `service/employee.service.ts` by executing the following command:

    $ cd src/app/ && mkdir models && mkdir services && cd models && touch employee.ts && cd ../services && touch employee.service.ts

5. Copy the following code to `angularjs-client/src/app/models/employee.ts`:

```
export class Employee
{
  constructor
  (
    public id: string,
    public firstName: string,
    public lastName: string
  ) {}
}
```

6. Copy the following code to `angularjs-client/src/app/services/employee.service.ts`:

```
import { Injectable } from '@angular/core';
import { Http, Response, Headers, RequestOptions } from
'@angular/http';
import { Observable } from 'rxjs/Rx';
import { Employee } from "app/models/employee";

@Injectable()
export class EmployeeService
{
  constructor(private http: Http) { }
  getEmployees(): Observable<Employee[]>
  {
    return this.http.get("http://localhost:8080/employees")
    .map((res: Response) => res.json())
    .catch((error: any) => Observable.throw(error.json().
    error || 'Server error'));
  }
```

```
addEmployee(employee: Employee): Observable<Employee>
{
  let headers = new Headers({ 'Content-Type':
  'application/json' });
  let options = new RequestOptions({ headers: headers });
  return this.http.post("http://localhost:8080/employee
  /add", employee, options)
  .map(this.extractData)
  .catch(this.handleErrorObservable);
}
private extractData(res: Response)
{
  let body = res.json();
  return body || {};
}
private handleErrorObservable(error: Response | any)
{
  console.error(error.message || error);
  return Observable.throw(error.message || error);
}
}
```

7. Replace the code of `angularjs-client/src/app/app.component.html` with the following:

```
<div class = "container" style="padding:5px">
  <form>
    <div class = "form-group">
      <label for = "id">ID</label>
      <input type = "text" class = "form-control" id = "id"
      required [(ngModel)] = "employee.id" name = "id">
    </div>
    <div class = "form-group">
      <label for = "firstName">FirstName</label>
      <input type = "text" class = "form-control" id =
      "firstName" [(ngModel)] = "employee.firstName" name =
      "firstName">
    </div>
    <div class = "form-group">
      <label for = "lastName">LastName</label>
      <input type = "text" class = "form-control" id =
      "lastName" [(ngModel)] = "employee.lastName" name =
      "lastName">
    </div>
    <div>
      <button (click)="addEmployee()">Add</button>
    </div>
```

```
      </form>
    </div>
    <table>
      <thead>
        <th>ID</th>
        <th>FirstName</th>
        <th>LastName</th>
      </thead>
      <tbody>
        <tr *ngFor="let employee of employees">
          <td>{{employee.id}}</td>
          <td>{{employee.firstName}}</td>
          <td>{{employee.lastName}}</td>
        </tr>
      </tbody>
    </table>
```

8. Replace the code of `angularjs-client/src/app/app.component.ts` with the following:

```
import { Component, OnInit } from '@angular/core';
import { EmployeeService } from "app/services/employee.service";
import { Employee } from './models/employee';

@Component
({
  selector: 'app-root',
  templateUrl: './app.component.html',
  styleUrls: ['./app.component.css'],
})
export class AppComponent implements OnInit
{
  title = 'app';
  employee = new Employee('', '', '');
  employees;
  constructor(private employeeService: EmployeeService) { }
  ngOnInit(): void
  {
    this.getEmployees();
  }
  getEmployees(): void
  {
    this.employeeService.getEmployees()
    .subscribe(employees => this.employees = employees);
  }
  addEmployee(): void
  {
```

```
      this.employeeService.addEmployee(this.employee)
      .subscribe
      (
        employee =>
        {
          this.getEmployees();
          this.reset();
        }
      );
  }
  private reset()
  {
    this.employee.id = null;
    this.employee.firstName = null;
    this.employee.lastName = null;
  }
}
```

9. Replace the code of `angularjs-client/src/app/app.module.ts` with the following:

```
import { BrowserModule } from '@angular/platform-browser';
import { NgModule } from '@angular/core';
import { HttpModule } from '@angular/http';
import { AppComponent } from './app.component';
import { EmployeeService } from "app/services/employee.service";
import { FormsModule } from '@angular/forms';

@NgModule
({
 declarations:
 [
   AppComponent
 ],
 imports:
 [
   BrowserModule, HttpModule, FormsModule
 ],
 providers: [EmployeeService],
 bootstrap: [AppComponent]
})
export class AppModule { }
```

With everything in place, the directory structure should look like the following:

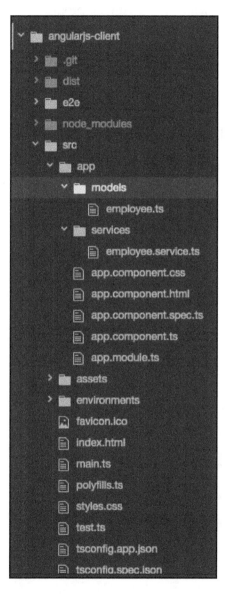

10. Move to the `angularjs-client` directory and execute the following commands to build the project artifacts and run the program:

```
$ ng build
$ go run server.go
```

How it works...

Once we run the program, the HTTP server will start locally listening on port 8080.

Browsing to `http://localhost:8080` will show us the AngularJS client page, which has an HTML form with **Id**, **FirstName**, and **LastName** fields, as shown in the following screenshot:

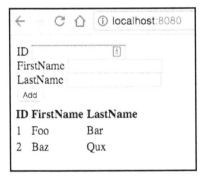

Clicking on the **Add** button after filling in the form will send a POST request to an HTTP server running on port 8080. Once a request is processed by the server it will return a list of all the static employees along with the newly added one, and display it in a browser, as shown in the following screenshot:

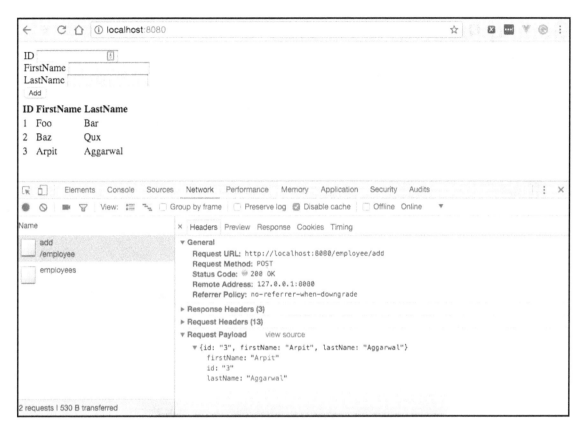

List of all the static employees along with the newly added one

Creating your first ReactJS client

ReactJS is a declarative JavaScript library that helps in building user interfaces efficiently. Because it works on the concept of virtual DOM it improves application performance, since JavaScript virtual DOM is faster than the regular DOM.

In this recipe, we will learn to create a ReactJS client to send a POST request to the HTTP server running locally.

Getting ready...

As we have already created an HTTP server that accepts both GET and POST HTTP requests in our previous recipe, we will be using the same code base as our HTTP server.

Also, this recipe assumes you have npm installed on your machine and you have basic knowledge of npm and webpack, which is a JavaScript Module bundler.

 See the *Creating your first HTTP POST method* recipe.

How to do it...

1. Create a reactjs-client directory where we will keep all our ReactJS source files and an HTTP server, as follows:

   ```
   $ mkdir reactjs-client && cd reactjs-client && touch server.go
   ```

2. Copy the following code to server.go:

   ```go
   package main
   import
   (
     "encoding/json"
     "log"
     "net/http"
     "github.com/gorilla/mux"
   )
   const
   (
     CONN_HOST = "localhost"
     CONN_PORT = "8080"
   )
   type Route struct
   {
     Name string
     Method string
     Pattern string
     HandlerFunc http.HandlerFunc
   }
   type Routes []Route
   var routes = Routes
   ```

```go
{
  Route
  {
    "getEmployees",
    "GET",
    "/employees",
    getEmployees,
  },
  Route
  {
    "addEmployee",
    "POST",
    "/employee/add",
    addEmployee,
  },
}
type Employee struct
{
  Id string `json:"id"`
  FirstName string `json:"firstName"`
  LastName string `json:"lastName"`
}
type Employees []Employee
var employees []Employee
func init()
{
  employees = Employees
  {
    Employee{Id: "1", FirstName: "Foo", LastName: "Bar"},
    Employee{Id: "2", FirstName: "Baz", LastName: "Qux"},
  }
}
func getEmployees(w http.ResponseWriter, r *http.Request)
{
  json.NewEncoder(w).Encode(employees)
}
func addEmployee(w http.ResponseWriter, r *http.Request)
{
  employee := Employee{}
  err := json.NewDecoder(r.Body).Decode(&employee)
  if err != nil
  {
    log.Print("error occurred while decoding employee
    data :: ", err)
    return
  }
  log.Printf("adding employee id :: %s with firstName
  as :: %s and lastName as :: %s ", employee.Id,
```

```go
      employee.FirstName, employee.LastName)
    employees = append(employees, Employee{Id: employee.Id,
    FirstName: employee.FirstName, LastName: employee.LastName})
    json.NewEncoder(w).Encode(employees)
}
func AddRoutes(router *mux.Router) *mux.Router
{
  for _, route := range routes
  {
    router.
    Methods(route.Method).
    Path(route.Pattern).
    Name(route.Name).
    Handler(route.HandlerFunc)
  }
  return router
}
func main()
{
  muxRouter := mux.NewRouter().StrictSlash(true)
  router := AddRoutes(muxRouter)
  router.PathPrefix("/").Handler(http.FileServer
  (http.Dir("./assets/")))
  err := http.ListenAndServe(CONN_HOST+":"+CONN_PORT, router)
  if err != nil
  {
    log.Fatal("error starting http server :: ", err)
    return
  }
}
```

3. Create another directory with the name `assets` where all our frontend code files, such as `.html`, `.js`, `.css`, and `images` will be kept, as follows:

   $ mkdir assets && cd assets && touch index.html

4. Copy the following content to `index.html`:

```html
<html>
  <head lang="en">
    <meta charset="UTF-8" />
    <title>ReactJS Client</title>
  </head>
  <body>
    <div id="react"></div>
    <script src="/script.js"></script>
```

```
    </body>
  </html>
```

5. Move to the `reactjs-client` directory and execute `npm init` to create `package.json` where we specify all the dependencies required to build our react client such as `React`, `React DOM`, `Webpack`, `Babel Loader`, `Babel Core`, `Babel Preset: ES2015`, and `Babel Preset: React`, as follows:

   $ cd reactjs-client && touch npm init

   Replace the content of `package.json` with the following content:

```json
{
  "name": "reactjs-client",
  "version": "1.0.0",
  "description": "ReactJs Client",
  "keywords":
  [
    "react"
  ],
  "author": "Arpit Aggarwal",
  "dependencies":
  {
    "axios": "^0.18.0",
    "react": "^16.2.0",
    "react-dom": "^16.2.0",
    "react-router-dom": "^4.2.2",
    "webpack": "^4.2.0",
    "webpack-cli": "^2.0.9",
    "lodash": "^4.17.5"
  },
  "scripts":
  {
    "build": "webpack",
    "watch": "webpack --watch -d"
  },
  "devDependencies":
  {
    "babel-core": "^6.18.2",
    "babel-loader": "^7.1.4",
    "babel-polyfill": "^6.16.0",
    "babel-preset-es2015": "^6.18.0",
    "babel-preset-react": "^6.16.0"
  }
}
```

6. Create `webpack.config.js` where we will configure `webpack`, as follows:

```
$ cd reactjs-client && touch webpack.config.js
```

Copy the following content to `webpack.config.js`:

```
var path = require('path');
module.exports =
{
  resolve:
  {
    extensions: ['.js', '.jsx']
  },
  mode: 'development',
  entry: './app/main.js',
  cache: true,
  output:
  {
    path: __dirname,
    filename: './assets/script.js'
  },
  module:
  {
    rules:
    [
      {
        test: path.join(__dirname, '.'),
        exclude: /(node_modules)/,
        loader: 'babel-loader',
        query:
        {
          cacheDirectory: true,
          presets: ['es2015', 'react']
        }
      }
    ]
  }
};
```

7. Create an entry point for the `webpack`, which is `reactjs-client/app/main.js` by executing the following commands:

```
$ cd reactjs-client && mkdir app && cd app && touch main.js
```

Copy the following content to `main.js`:

```
'use strict';
const React = require('react');
const ReactDOM = require('react-dom')
import EmployeeApp from './components/employee-app.jsx'
ReactDOM.render
(
  <EmployeeApp />,
  document.getElementById('react')
)
```

8. Define `ReactApp` along with its child components by executing the following commands:

```
$ cd reactjs-client && mkdir components && cd components && touch
react-app.jsx employee-list.jsx employee.jsx add-employee.jsx
```

Copy the following content to `reactjs-client/app/components/employee-app.jsx`:

```
'use strict';
const React = require('react');
var axios = require('axios');
import EmployeeList from './employee-list.jsx'
import AddEmployee from './add-employee.jsx'
export default class EmployeeApp extends React.Component
{
  constructor(props)
  {
    super(props);
    this.state = {employees: []};
    this.addEmployee = this.addEmployee.bind(this);
    this.Axios = axios.create
    (
      {
        headers: {'content-type': 'application/json'}
      }
    );
  }
  componentDidMount()
  {
    let _this = this;
    this.Axios.get('/employees')
    .then
    (
      function (response)
```

```
        {
          _this.setState({employees: response.data});
        }
      )
      .catch(function (error) { });
    }
    addEmployee(employeeName)
    {
      let _this = this;
      this.Axios.post
      (
        '/employee/add',
        {
          firstName: employeeName
        }
      )
      .then
      (
        function (response)
        {
          _this.setState({employees: response.data});
        }
      )
      .catch(function (error) { });
    }
    render()
    {
      return
      (
        <div>
          <AddEmployee addEmployee={this.addEmployee}/>
          <EmployeeList employees={this.state.employees}/>
        </div>
      )
    }
  }
```

Copy the following content to `reactjs-client/app/components/employee.jsx`:

```
const React = require('react');
export default class Employee extends React.Component
{
  render()
  {
    return
    (
```

```
    <tr>
      <td>{this.props.employee.firstName}</td>
    </tr>
  )
 }
}
```

Copy the following content to `reactjs-client/app/components/employee-list.jsx`:

```
const React = require('react');
import Employee from './employee.jsx'
export default class EmployeeList extends React.Component
{
  render()
  {
    var employees = this.props.employees.map
    (
      (employee, i) =>
      <Employee key={i} employee={employee}/>
    );
    return
    (
      <table>
        <tbody>
          <tr>
            <th>FirstName</th>
          </tr>
          {employees}
        </tbody>
      </table>
    )
  }
}
```

Copy the following content to `reactjs-client/app/components/add-employee.jsx`:

```
import React, { Component, PropTypes } from 'react'
export default class AddEmployee extends React.Component
{
  render()
  {
    return
    (
      <div>
        <input type = 'text' ref = 'input' />
```

```
                <button onClick = {(e) => this.handleClick(e)}>
                  Add
                </button>
              </div>
            )
          }
          handleClick(e)
          {
            const node = this.refs.input
            const text = node.value.trim()
            this.props.addEmployee(text)
            node.value = ''
          }
        }
```

With everything in place, the directory structure should look like the following:

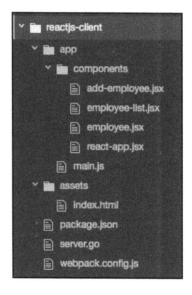

Directory structure

9. Move to the `reactjs-client` directory and execute the following commands to install `node modules` and build `webpack`:

```
$ npm install
$ npm run build
```

10. Run the program with the following command:

```
$ go run server.go
```

How it works...

Once we run the program, the HTTP server will start locally listening on port `8080`.

Browsing to `http://localhost:8080` will show us the ReactJS client page, as shown in the following screenshot:

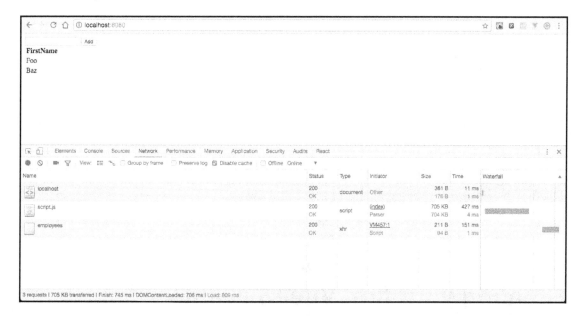

ReactJS client page

Clicking on the **Add** button after filling in the textbox will send a `POST` request to the HTTP server running on port `8080`:

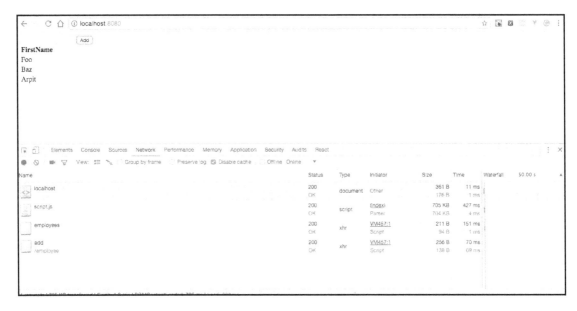

Click on the Add button after filling in the textbox

Next, executing a `GET` request from the command line as follows will give you a list of all the static employees:

```
$ curl -X GET http://localhost:8080/employees
```

This will be alongside the newly added one, as follows:

```
[{"id":"1","firstName":"Foo","lastName":"Bar"},{"id":"2","firstName":"Baz",
"lastName":"Qux"},{"id":"","firstName":"Arpit","lastName":""}]
```

Creating your first VueJS client

Being open source, VueJS is one of the incrementally adoptable and progressive JavaScript frameworks that companies are adopting to build their frontend or client-facing user interfaces for the web.

In this recipe, we will learn to create a client in VueJS, which adds an employee sending an HTTP `POST` request to the HTTP server running locally.

Getting ready...

As we have already created an HTTP server that accepts both GET and POST requests in one of our previous recipes, we will be using the same code base as our HTTP server.

See the *Creating your first HTTP POST method* recipe.

How to do it...

1. Create a vuejs-client directory where we will keep all our VueJS source files and an HTTP server, as follows:

   ```
   $ mkdir vuejs-client && cd vuejs-client && touch server.go
   ```

2. Copy the following code to server.go:

   ```
   package main
   import
   (
     "encoding/json"
     "log"
     "net/http"
     "github.com/gorilla/mux"
   )
   const
   (
     CONN_HOST = "localhost"
     CONN_PORT = "8080"
   )
   type Route struct
   {
     Name string
     Method string
     Pattern string
     HandlerFunc http.HandlerFunc
   }
   type Routes []Route
   var routes = Routes
   {
     Route
     {
   ```

```
        "getEmployees",
        "GET",
        "/employees",
        getEmployees,
      },
      Route
      {
        "addEmployee",
        "POST",
        "/employee/add",
        addEmployee,
      },
  }
  type Employee struct
  {
    Id string `json:"id"`
    FirstName string `json:"firstName"`
    LastName string `json:"lastName"`
  }
  type Employees []Employee
  var employees []Employee
  func init()
  {
    employees = Employees
    {
      Employee{Id: "1", FirstName: "Foo", LastName: "Bar"},
      Employee{Id: "2", FirstName: "Baz", LastName: "Qux"},
    }
  }
  func getEmployees(w http.ResponseWriter, r *http.Request)
  {
    json.NewEncoder(w).Encode(employees)
  }
  func addEmployee(w http.ResponseWriter, r *http.Request)
  {
    employee := Employee{}
    err := json.NewDecoder(r.Body).Decode(&employee)
    if err != nil
    {
      log.Print("error occurred while decoding employee
      data :: ", err)
      return
    }
    log.Printf("adding employee id :: %s with firstName
    as :: %s and lastName as :: %s ", employee.Id,
    employee.FirstName, employee.LastName)
    employees = append(employees, Employee{Id: employee.Id,
    FirstName: employee.FirstName, LastName: employee.LastName})
```

```
    json.NewEncoder(w).Encode(employees)
}
func AddRoutes(router *mux.Router) *mux.Router
{
  for _, route := range routes
  {
    router.
    Methods(route.Method).
    Path(route.Pattern).
    Name(route.Name).
    Handler(route.HandlerFunc)
  }
  return router
}
func main()
{
  muxRouter := mux.NewRouter().StrictSlash(true)
  router := AddRoutes(muxRouter)
  router.PathPrefix("/").Handler(http.FileServer
  (http.Dir("./assets/")))
  err := http.ListenAndServe(CONN_HOST+":"+CONN_PORT, router)
  if err != nil
  {
    log.Fatal("error starting http server :: ", err)
    return
  }
}
```

3. Create another directory with the name `assets` where all our frontend code files such as `.html`, `.js`, `.css`, and `images` will be kept, as follows:

   $ mkdir assets && cd assets && touch index.html && touch main.js

4. Copy the following content to `index.html`:

```
<html>
  <head>
    <title>VueJs Client</title>
    <script type = "text/javascript" src = "https://cdnjs.
    cloudflare.com/ajax/libs/vue/2.4.0/vue.js"></script>
    <script type = "text/javascript" src="https://cdn.
    jsdelivr.net/npm/vue-resource@1.5.0"></script>
  </head>
  <body>
    <div id = "form">
      <h1>{{ message }}</h1>
      <table>
```

```
          <tr>
            <td><label for="id">Id</label></td>
            <td><input type="text" value="" v-model="id"/></td>
          </tr>
          <tr>
            <td><label for="firstName">FirstName</label></td>
            <td><input type="text" value="" v-model="firstName"/>
            <td>
          </tr>
          <tr>
            <td><label for="lastName">LastName</label></td>
            <td> <input type="text" value="" v-model="lastName" />
            </td>
          </tr>
          <tr>
            <td><a href="#" class="btn" @click="addEmployee">Add
            </a></td>
          </tr>
        </table>
      </div>
      <script type = "text/javascript" src = "main.js"></script>
    </body>
  </html>
```

5. Copy the following content to `main.js`:

```
var vue_det = new Vue
({
 el: '#form',
 data:
 {
   message: 'Employee Dashboard',
   id: '',
   firstName:'',
   lastName:''
 },
 methods:
 {
   addEmployee: function()
   {
     this.$http.post
     (
       '/employee/add',
       {
         id: this.id,
         firstName:this.firstName,
         lastName:this.lastName
       }
```

```
      )
      .then
      (
        response =>
        {
          console.log(response);
        },
        error =>
        {
          console.error(error);
        }
      );
    }
  }
});
```

With everything in place, the directory structure should look like the following:

Directory structure

6. Run the program with the following command:

```
$ go run server.go
```

How it works...

Once we run the program, the HTTP server will start locally listening on port 8080.

Browsing to http://localhost:8080 will show us the VueJS client page, which has an HTML form with **Id**, **FirstName**, and **LastName** fields, as shown in the following screenshot:

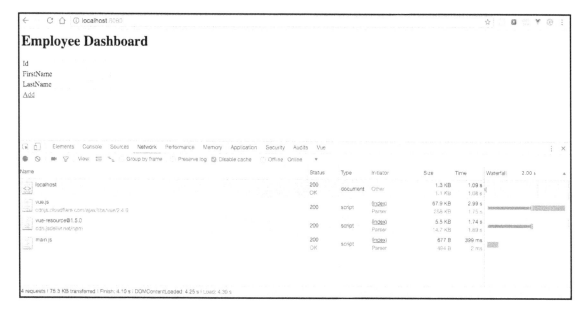

VueJS client page

Clicking on the **Add** button after filling in the form will send a POST request to the HTTP server running on port 8080, as shown in the following screenshot:

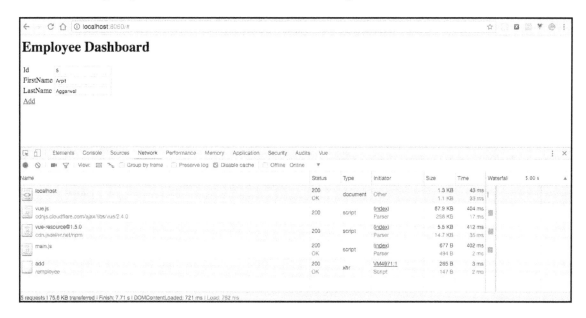

Click on the Add button after filling in the form

Next, executing a GET request from the command line as follows, will give you a list of all the static employees:

```
$ curl -X GET http://localhost:8080/employees
```

This will be alongside the newly added one as follows:

```
[{"id":"1","firstName":"Foo","lastName":"Bar"},{"id":"2","firstName":"Baz",
"lastName":"Qux"},{"id":"5","firstName":"Arpit","lastName":"Aggarwal"}]
```

Working with SQL and NoSQL Databases

5

In this chapter, we will cover the following recipes:

- Integrating MySQL and Go
- Creating your first record in MySQL
- Reading records from MySQL
- Updating your first record in MySQL
- Deleting your first record from MySQL
- Integrating MongoDB and Go
- Creating your first document in MongoDB
- Reading documents from MongoDB
- Updating your first document in MongoDB
- Deleting your first document from MongoDB

Introduction

Whenever we want to persist data we always look forward to saving it in databases, which are mainly divided into two categories—**SQL** and **NoSQL**. There are a number of databases under each category that can be used depending on the business use case because each one has different characteristics and serves a different purpose.

In this chapter, we will integrate a Go web application with the most famous open source databases—**MySQL** and **MongoDB** and learn to perform CRUD operations on them. As we will use MySQL and MongoDB, I assume both of the databases are installed and running on your local machine.

Integrating MySQL and Go

Let's assume you are a developer and want to save your application data in a MySQL database. As a first step, you have to establish a connection between your application and MySQL, which we will cover in this recipe.

Getting ready...

Verify whether MySQL is installed and running locally on port 3306 by executing the following command:

```
$ ps -ef | grep 3306
```

This should return the following response:

```
   ps -ef | grep 3306
502  5690  2458   0  7:12PM ttys004   0:00.00 grep --color=auto --exclude-dir=.bzr --exclude-dir=CVS --exclude-dir=.git --exclude-dir=.hg --exclude-dir=.svn 3306
```

Also, log into the MySQL database and create a mydb database, executing the commands as shown in the following screenshot:

```
     mysql -u root -ppassword
mysql: [Warning] Using a password on the command line interface can be insecure.
Welcome to the MySQL monitor.  Commands end with ; or \g.
Your MySQL connection id is 9
Server version: 5.7.21 Homebrew

Copyright (c) 2000, 2018, Oracle and/or its affiliates. All rights reserved.

Oracle is a registered trademark of Oracle Corporation and/or its
affiliates. Other names may be trademarks of their respective
owners.

Type 'help;' or '\h' for help. Type '\c' to clear the current input statement.

mysql> create database mydb;
Query OK, 1 row affected (0.00 sec)

mysql> commit;
Query OK, 0 rows affected (0.00 sec)

mysql>
```

How to do it...

1. Install the `github.com/go-sql-driver/mysql` package, using the `go get` command, as follows:

   ```
   $ go get github.com/go-sql-driver/mysql
   ```

2. Create `connect-mysql.go`. Then we connect to the MySQL database and perform a `SELECT` query to get the current database name, as follows:

   ```go
   package main
   import
   (
     "database/sql"
     "fmt"
     "log"
     "net/http"
     "github.com/go-sql-driver/mysql"
   )
   const
   (
     CONN_HOST = "localhost"
     CONN_PORT = "8080"
     DRIVER_NAME = "mysql"
     DATA_SOURCE_NAME = "root:password@/mydb"
   )
   var db *sql.DB
   var connectionError error
   func init()
   {
     db, connectionError = sql.Open(DRIVER_NAME, DATA_SOURCE_NAME)
     if connectionError != nil
     {
       log.Fatal("error connecting to database :: ", connectionError)
     }
   }
   func getCurrentDb(w http.ResponseWriter, r *http.Request)
   {
     rows, err := db.Query("SELECT DATABASE() as db")
     if err != nil
     {
       log.Print("error executing query :: ", err)
       return
     }
     var db string
     for rows.Next()
   ```

```
        {
          rows.Scan(&db)
        }
        fmt.Fprintf(w, "Current Database is :: %s", db)
      }
      func main()
      {
        http.HandleFunc("/", getCurrentDb)
        defer db.Close()
        err := http.ListenAndServe(CONN_HOST+":"+CONN_PORT, nil)
        if err != nil
        {
          log.Fatal("error starting http server :: ", err)
          return
        }
      }
```

3. Run the program with the following command:

```
$ go run connect-mysql.go
```

How it works...

Once we run the program, the HTTP server will start locally listening on port 8080.

Browsing to http://localhost:8080/ will return you the current database name, as shown in the following screenshot:

Let's understand the program we have written:

1. Using import ("database/sql" "fmt" "log" "net/http" _ "github.com/go-sql-driver/mysql"), we imported github.com/go-sql-driver/mysql for its side effects or initialization, using the underscore in front of an import statement explicitly.

2. Using `var db *sql.DB`, we declared a private `DB` instance.

 Depending on the project size, you can declare a DB instance globally, inject it as a dependency using handlers, or put the connection pool pointer into `x/net/context`.

3. Next, we defined an `init()` function where we connect to the database passing the database driver name and data source to it.
4. Then, we defined a `getCurrentDb` handler, which basically performs a select query on the database to get the current database name, iterates over the records, copies its value into the variable, and eventually writes it to an HTTP response stream.

Creating your first record in MySQL

Creating or saving a record in a database requires us to write SQL queries and execute them, implement **object-relational mapping (ORM)**, or implement data-mapping techniques.

In this recipe, we will be writing a SQL query and executing it using the `database/sql` package to create a record. To achieve this, you can also implement ORM using any library from a number of third-party libraries available in Go, such as `https://github.com/jinzhu/gorm`, `https://github.com/go-gorp/gorp`, and `https://github.com/jirfag/go-queryset`.

Getting ready...

As we have already established a connection with the MySQL database in our previous recipe, we will just extend it to create a record executing a SQL query.

Before creating a record, we have to create a table in the MySQL database, which we will do by executing the commands shown in the following screenshot:

```
      mysql -u root -ppassword
mysql: [Warning] Using a password on the command line interface can be insecure.
Welcome to the MySQL monitor.  Commands end with ; or \g.
Your MySQL connection id is 10
Server version: 5.7.21 Homebrew

Copyright (c) 2000, 2018, Oracle and/or its affiliates. All rights reserved.

Oracle is a registered trademark of Oracle Corporation and/or its
affiliates. Other names may be trademarks of their respective
owners.

Type 'help;' or '\h' for help. Type '\c' to clear the current input statement.

mysql> use mydb;
Database changed
mysql> CREATE TABLE employee (uid INT(10) NOT NULL AUTO_INCREMENT, name VARCHAR(64) NULL DEFAULT NULL, PRIMARY KEY (uid));
Query OK, 0 rows affected (0.09 sec)

mysql> commit;
Query OK, 0 rows affected (0.00 sec)

mysql>
```

How to do it...

1. Install the `github.com/go-sql-driver/mysql` and `github.com/gorilla/mux` packages, using the `go get` command, as follows:

```
$ go get github.com/go-sql-driver/mysql
$ go get github.com/gorilla/mux
```

2. Create `create-record-mysql.go`. Then we connect to the MySQL database and perform an INSERT query to create an employee record, as follows:

```
package main
import
(
  "database/sql"
  "fmt"
  "log"
  "net/http"
  "strconv"
  "github.com/go-sql-driver/mysql"
  "github.com/gorilla/mux"
)
const
(
```

```go
    CONN_HOST = "localhost"
    CONN_PORT = "8080"
    DRIVER_NAME = "mysql"
    DATA_SOURCE_NAME = "root:password@/mydb"
)
var db *sql.DB
var connectionError error
func init()
{
    db, connectionError = sql.Open(DRIVER_NAME, DATA_SOURCE_NAME)
    if connectionError != nil
    {
        log.Fatal("error connecting to database : ", connectionError)
    }
}
func createRecord(w http.ResponseWriter, r *http.Request)
{
    vals := r.URL.Query()
    name, ok := vals["name"]
    if ok
    {
        log.Print("going to insert record in database for name : ",
        name[0])
        stmt, err := db.Prepare("INSERT employee SET name=?")
        if err != nil
        {
            log.Print("error preparing query :: ", err)
            return
        }
        result, err := stmt.Exec(name[0])
        if err != nil
        {
            log.Print("error executing query :: ", err)
            return
        }
        id, err := result.LastInsertId()
        fmt.Fprintf(w, "Last Inserted Record Id is :: %s",
        strconv.FormatInt(id, 10))
    }
    else
    {
        fmt.Fprintf(w, "Error occurred while creating record in
        database for name :: %s", name[0])
    }
}
func main()
{
    router := mux.NewRouter()
```

```
router.HandleFunc("/employee/create", createRecord).
Methods("POST")
defer db.Close()
err := http.ListenAndServe(CONN_HOST+":"+CONN_PORT, router)
if err != nil
{
  log.Fatal("error starting http server : ", err)
  return
}
}
```

3. Run the program with the following command:

```
$ go run create-record-mysql.go
```

How it works...

Once we run the program, the HTTP server will start locally listening on port 8080.

Executing a POST request to create an employee record from the command line as follows will give you the ID of the last record created:

```
$ curl -X POST http://localhost:8080/employee/create?name=foo
Last created record id is :: 1
```

Let's understand the program we have written:

1. Using import ("database/sql" "fmt" "log" "net/http" "strconv" _ "github.com/go-sql-driver/mysql" "github.com/gorilla/mux"), we imported github.com/gorilla/mux to create a Gorilla Mux Router and initialized the Go MySQL driver, importing the github.com/go-sql-driver/mysql package.

2. Next, we defined a createRecord handler, which fetches the name from the request, assigns it to the local variable name, prepares an INSERT statement with a name placeholder that will be replaced dynamically with the name, executes the statement, and eventually writes the last created ID to an HTTP response stream.

Reading records from MySQL

In the previous recipe, we created an employee record in the MySQL database. Now, in this recipe, we will learn how we can read it by executing a SQL query.

How to do it...

1. Install the `github.com/go-sql-driver/mysql` and `github.com/gorilla/mux` packages using the `go get` command, as follows:

```
$ go get github.com/go-sql-driver/mysql
$ go get github.com/gorilla/mux
```

2. Create `read-record-mysql.go` where we connect to the MySQL database, perform a `SELECT` query to get all the employees from the database, iterate over the records, copy its value into the struct, add all of them to a list, and write it to an HTTP response stream, as follows:

```
package main
import
(
  "database/sql" "encoding/json"
  "log"
  "net/http"
  "github.com/go-sql-driver/mysql"
  "github.com/gorilla/mux"
)
const
(
  CONN_HOST = "localhost"
  CONN_PORT = "8080"
  DRIVER_NAME = "mysql"
  DATA_SOURCE_NAME = "root:password@/mydb"
)
var db *sql.DB
var connectionError error
func init()
{
  db, connectionError = sql.Open(DRIVER_NAME, DATA_SOURCE_NAME)
  if connectionError != nil
  {
    log.Fatal("error connecting to database :: ", connectionError)
  }
```

```
    }
    type Employee struct
    {
      Id int `json:"uid"`
      Name string `json:"name"`
    }
    func readRecords(w http.ResponseWriter, r *http.Request)
    {
      log.Print("reading records from database")
      rows, err := db.Query("SELECT * FROM employee")
      if err != nil
      {
        log.Print("error occurred while executing select
        query :: ",err)
        return
      }
      employees := []Employee{}
      for rows.Next()
      {
        var uid int
        var name string
        err = rows.Scan(&uid, &name)
        employee := Employee{Id: uid, Name: name}
        employees = append(employees, employee)
      }
      json.NewEncoder(w).Encode(employees)
    }
    func main()
    {
      router := mux.NewRouter()
      router.HandleFunc("/employees", readRecords).Methods("GET")
      defer db.Close()
      err := http.ListenAndServe(CONN_HOST+":"+CONN_PORT, router)
      if err != nil
      {
        log.Fatal("error starting http server :: ", err)
        return
      }
    }
```

3. Run the program with the following command:

```
$ go run read-record-mysql.go
```

How it works...

Once we run the program, the HTTP server will start locally listening on port 8080.

Browsing to `http://localhost:8080/employees` will list all the records from the employee table as shown in the following screenshot:

Let's look at the program we have written:

1. Using `import ( "database/sql" "encoding/json" "log" "net/http" _ "github.com/go-sql-driver/mysql" "github.com/gorilla/mux")`, we imported an additional package, `encoding/json`, which helps in marshalling the Go data structure to `JSON`.

2. Next, we declared the Go data structure `Person`, which has `Id` and `Name` fields.

Do remember that the field name should begin with a capital letter in the type definition or there could be errors.

3. Next, we defined a `readRecords` handler, which queries the database to get all the records from the employee table, iterates over the records, copies its value into the struct, adds all the records to a list, marshals the object list to JSON, and writes it to an HTTP response stream.

Updating your first record in MySQL

Consider a scenario where you have created a record for an employee in a database with all its details, such as name, department, address, and so on, and after some time the employee changes departments. In that case, we have to update their department in a database so that their details are in sync all across the organization, which can be achieved using a SQL UPDATE statement, and in this recipe we will learn how we can implement it in Go.

How to do it...

1. Install the github.com/go-sql-driver/mysql
   and github.com/gorilla/mux packages, using the go get command, as follows:

   ```
   $ go get github.com/go-sql-driver/mysql
   $ go get github.com/gorilla/mux
   ```

2. Create update-record-mysql.go. Then we connect to the MySQL database, update the name of an employee for an ID, and write the number of records updated in a database to an HTTP response stream, as follows:

   ```
   package main
   import
   (
     "database/sql"
     "fmt"
     "log"
     "net/http"
     "github.com/go-sql-driver/mysql"
     "github.com/gorilla/mux"
   )
   const
   (
     CONN_HOST = "localhost"
     CONN_PORT = "8080"
     DRIVER_NAME = "mysql"
     DATA_SOURCE_NAME = "root:password@/mydb"
   )
   var db *sql.DB
   var connectionError error
   func init()
   {
     db, connectionError = sql.Open(DRIVER_NAME, DATA_SOURCE_NAME)
   ```

```go
    if connectionError != nil
    {
      log.Fatal("error connecting to database :: ", connectionError)
    }
}
type Employee struct
{
  Id    int    `json:"uid"`
  Name string `json:"name"`
}
func updateRecord(w http.ResponseWriter, r *http.Request)
{
  vars := mux.Vars(r)
  id := vars["id"]
  vals := r.URL.Query()
  name, ok := vals["name"]
  if ok
  {
    log.Print("going to update record in database
    for id :: ", id)
    stmt, err := db.Prepare("UPDATE employee SET name=?
    where uid=?")
    if err != nil
    {
      log.Print("error occurred while preparing query :: ", err)
      return
    }
    result, err := stmt.Exec(name[0], id)
    if err != nil
    {
      log.Print("error occurred while executing query :: ", err)
      return
    }
    rowsAffected, err := result.RowsAffected()
    fmt.Fprintf(w, "Number of rows updated in database
    are :: %d",rowsAffected)
  }
  else
  {
    fmt.Fprintf(w, "Error occurred while updating record in
    database for id :: %s", id)
  }
}
func main()
{
  router := mux.NewRouter()
  router.HandleFunc("/employee/update/{id}",
  updateRecord).Methods("PUT")
```

```
      defer db.Close()
      err := http.ListenAndServe(CONN_HOST+":"+CONN_PORT, router)
      if err != nil
      {
        log.Fatal("error starting http server :: ", err)
        return
      }
    }
```

3. Run the program with the following command:

```
$ go run update-record-mysql.go
```

How it works...

Once we run the program, the HTTP server will start locally listening on port 8080.

Next, executing a PUT request from the command line to update an employee record with the ID as 1 will give you the number of records updated in the database as a response:

```
$ curl -X PUT http://localhost:8080/employee/update/1?name\=bar
Number of rows updated in database are :: 1
```

Let's look at the program we have written:

1. We defined an updateRecord handler, which gets the ID to be updated in the database as a URL path variable path, and the new name as the request variable, prepares an update statement with a name and UID as a placeholder, which will be replaced dynamically, executes the statement, gets the number of rows updated as a result of its execution, and writes it to an HTTP response stream.

2. Next, we registered an updateRecord handler to be called for the URL pattern /employee/update/{id} for every PUT request with the gorilla/mux router and closed the database using the defer db.Close() statement once we return from the main() function.

Deleting your first record from MySQL

Consider a scenario where an employee has left the organization and you want to revoke their details from the database. In that case, we can use the SQL DELETE statement, which we will be covering in this recipe.

How to do it...

1. Install the github.com/go-sql-driver/mysql and github.com/gorilla/mux packages, using the go get command, as follows:

   ```
   $ go get github.com/go-sql-driver/mysql
   $ go get github.com/gorilla/mux
   ```

2. Create delete-record-mysql.go. Then we connect to the MySQL database, delete the name of an employee from the database, and write the number of records deleted from a database to an HTTP response stream, as follows:

   ```
   package main
   import
   (
     "database/sql"
     "fmt"
     "log"
     "net/http"
     "github.com/go-sql-driver/mysql"
     "github.com/gorilla/mux"
   )
   const
   (
     CONN_HOST = "localhost"
     CONN_PORT = "8080"
     DRIVER_NAME = "mysql"
     DATA_SOURCE_NAME = "root:password@/mydb"
   )
   var db *sql.DB
   var connectionError error
   func init()
   {
     db, connectionError = sql.Open(DRIVER_NAME, DATA_SOURCE_NAME)
     if connectionError != nil
     {
       log.Fatal("error connecting to database :: ", connectionError)
   ```

```go
      }
  }
  func deleteRecord(w http.ResponseWriter, r *http.Request)
  {
    vals := r.URL.Query()
    name, ok := vals["name"]
    if ok
    {
      log.Print("going to delete record in database for
      name :: ", name[0])
      stmt, err := db.Prepare("DELETE from employee where name=?")
      if err != nil
      {
        log.Print("error occurred while preparing query :: ", err)
        return
      }
      result, err := stmt.Exec(name[0])
      if err != nil
      {
        log.Print("error occurred while executing query :: ", err)
        return
      }
      rowsAffected, err := result.RowsAffected()
      fmt.Fprintf(w, "Number of rows deleted in database are :: %d",
      rowsAffected)
    }
    else
    {
      fmt.Fprintf(w, "Error occurred while deleting record in
      database for name %s", name[0])
    }
  }
  func main()
  {
    router := mux.NewRouter()
    router.HandleFunc("/employee/delete",
    deleteRecord).Methods("DELETE")
    defer db.Close()
    err := http.ListenAndServe(CONN_HOST+":"+CONN_PORT, router)
    if err != nil
    {
      log.Fatal("error starting http server :: ", err)
      return
    }
  }
```

3. Run the program with the following command:

```
$ go run delete-record-mysql.go
```

How it works...

Once we run the program, the HTTP server will start locally listening on port 8080.

Next, executing a DELETE request from the command line to delete an employee with the name as bar will give you the number of records deleted from the database:

```
$ curl -X DELETE http://localhost:8080/employee/delete?name\=bar
Number of rows deleted in database are :: 1
```

Let's look at the program we have written:

1. We defined a deleteRecord handler, which gets the name to be deleted from the database as the request variable, prepares a DELETE statement with a name as a placeholder, which will be replaced dynamically, executes the statement, gets the count of rows deleted as a result of its execution, and writes it to an HTTP response stream.

2. Next, we registered a deleteRecord handler to be called for the URL pattern /employee/delete for every DELETE request with gorilla/mux router and closed the database using the defer db.Close() statement once we returned from the main() function.

Integrating MongoDB and Go

Whenever you want to persist data in a MongoDB database, the first step you have to take is to establish a connection between the database and your web application, which we will be covering in this recipe using one of the most famous and commonly used MongoDB drivers for Go - gopkg.in/mgo.v2.

Getting ready...

Verify whether MongoDB is installed and running locally on port 27017 by executing the following command:

```
$ mongo
```

This should return the following response:

```
        mongo
MongoDB shell version: 3.0.7
connecting to: test
Server has startup warnings:
2018-04-07T19:24:52.196+0530 I CONTROL  [initandlisten]
2018-04-07T19:24:52.196+0530 I CONTROL  [initandlisten] ** WARNING: soft rlimits too low. Number of files is 256, should be at least 1000
>
```

How to do it...

1. Install the gopkg.in/mgo.v package, using the go get command, as follows:

    ```
    $ go get gopkg.in/mgo.v
    ```

2. Create connect-mongodb.go. Then we connect to the MongoDB database, get all the database names from the cluster, and write them to an HTTP response stream, as follows:

    ```
    package main
    import
    (
      "fmt"
      "log"
      "net/http"
      "strings"
      mgo "gopkg.in/mgo.v2"
    )
    const
    (
      CONN_HOST = "localhost"
      CONN_PORT = "8080"
      MONGO_DB_URL = "127.0.0.1"
    )
    var session *mgo.Session
    var connectionError error
    func init()
    {
    ```

```
    session, connectionError = mgo.Dial(MONGO_DB_URL)
    if connectionError != nil
    {
      log.Fatal("error connecting to database :: ", connectionError)
    }
    session.SetMode(mgo.Monotonic, true)
}
func getDbNames(w http.ResponseWriter, r *http.Request)
{
  db, err := session.DatabaseNames()
  if err != nil
  {
    log.Print("error getting database names :: ", err)
    return
  }
  fmt.Fprintf(w, "Databases names are :: %s", strings.Join
  (db, ", "))
}
func main()
{
  http.HandleFunc("/", getDbNames)
  defer session.Close()
  err := http.ListenAndServe(CONN_HOST+":"+CONN_PORT, nil)
  if err != nil
  {
    log.Fatal("error starting http server :: ", err)
    return
  }
}
```

3. Run the program with the following command:

```
$ go run connect-mongodb.go
```

How it works...

Once we run the program, the HTTP server will start locally listening on port 8080.

Browsing to `http://localhost:8080/` will list you the name of all the databases that exist in the MongoDB cluster and will look as shown in the following screenshot:

Let's look at the program we have written:

1. Using `import ( "fmt" "log" "net/http" "strings" mgo "gopkg.in/mgo.v2" )`, we imported `gopkg.in/mgo.v2` with the package alias name as `mgo`.
2. Using `var session *mgo.Session`, we declared the private MongoDB `Session` instance, which acts as a communication session with the database.
3. Using `var connectionError error`, we declared a private `error` object.
4. Next, we defined the `init()` function, where we connected to MongoDB, passing the host as `127.0.0.1`, which means both MongoDB and the application are running on the same machine at port `27017`, optionally switching the session to a monotonic behavior so that the read data will be consistent across sequential queries in the same session, and modifications made within the session will be observed in the queries that follow.

 If your MongoDB is running on a port other than `27017`, then you have to pass both the host and port separated by a colon, as: `mgo.Dial("localhost:27018")`.

5. Next, we defined a `getDbNames` handler, which basically gets all the database names from the MongoDB cluster and writes them to an HTTP response stream as a comma-separated string.

Creating your first document in MongoDB

In this recipe, we will learn how we can create a BSON document (a binary-encoded serialization of JSON-like documents) in a database, using a MongoDB driver for Go (gopkg.in/mgo.v2).

How to do it...

1. Install the gopkg.in/mgo.v2 and github.com/gorilla/mux packages, using the go get command, as follows:

```
$ go get gopkg.in/mgo.v2
$ go get github.com/gorilla/mux
```

2. Create create-record-mongodb.go. Then we connect to the MongoDB database, create an employee document with two fields—ID and name—and write the last created document ID to an HTTP response stream, as follows:

```go
package main
import
(
  "fmt"
  "log"
  "net/http"
  "strconv"
  "github.com/gorilla/mux"
  mgo "gopkg.in/mgo.v2"
)
const
(
  CONN_HOST = "localhost"
  CONN_PORT = "8080"
  MONGO_DB_URL = "127.0.0.1"
)
var session *mgo.Session
var connectionError error
type Employee struct
{
  Id int `json:"uid"`
  Name string `json:"name"`
}
func init()
{
  session, connectionError = mgo.Dial(MONGO_DB_URL)
```

```go
   if connectionError != nil
   {
     log.Fatal("error connecting to database :: ", connectionError)
   }
   session.SetMode(mgo.Monotonic, true)
}
func createDocument(w http.ResponseWriter, r *http.Request)
{
   vals := r.URL.Query()
   name, nameOk := vals["name"]
   id, idOk := vals["id"]
   if nameOk && idOk
   {
     employeeId, err := strconv.Atoi(id[0])
     if err != nil
     {
       log.Print("error converting string id to int :: ", err)
       return
     }
     log.Print("going to insert document in database for name
     :: ", name[0])
     collection := session.DB("mydb").C("employee")
     err = collection.Insert(&Employee{employeeId, name[0]})
     if err != nil
     {
       log.Print("error occurred while inserting document in
       database :: ", err)
       return
     }
     fmt.Fprintf(w, "Last created document id is :: %s", id[0])
   }
   else
   {
     fmt.Fprintf(w, "Error occurred while creating document in
     database for name :: %s", name[0])
   }
}
func main()
{
   router := mux.NewRouter()
   router.HandleFunc("/employee/create",
   createDocument).Methods("POST")
   defer session.Close()
   err := http.ListenAndServe(CONN_HOST+":"+CONN_PORT, router)
   if err != nil
   {
     log.Fatal("error starting http server :: ", err)
     return
```

```
      }
    }
```

3. Run the program with the following command:

```
$ go run create-record-mongodb.go
```

How it works...

Once we run the program, the HTTP server will start locally listening on port 8080.

Next, executing a POST request to create an employee document from the command line as follows will give you the ID of the document created in MongoDB:

```
$ curl -X POST http://localhost:8080/employee/create?name=foo\&id=1
Last created document id is :: 1
```

Let's look at the program we have written:

1. Using import ("fmt" "log" "net/http" "strconv"
   "github.com/gorilla/mux" mgo "gopkg.in/mgo.v2"), we imported
   github.com/gorilla/mux to create a Gorilla Mux Router and
   gopkg.in/mgo.v2 with the package alias name as mgo, which will act as a
   MongoDB driver.

2. Next, we defined a createDocument handler, which fetches the name and ID of
   an employee from the HTTP request. Because request variables are of type
   string, we converted the variable ID of string type to int type. Then, we get
   the employee collection from MongoDB and call the collection.Insert
   handler to save an instance of the Employee struct type in the database.

Reading documents from MongoDB

In the previous recipe, we created a BSON document in MongoDB. Now, in this recipe, we will learn how to read it using the gopkg.in/mgo.v2/bson package, which helps to query the MongoDB collection.

How to do it...

1. Install the `gopkg.in/mgo.v2`, `gopkg.in/mgo.v2/bson`, and `github.com/gorilla/mux` packages, using the `go get` command, as follows:

```
$ go get gopkg.in/mgo.v2
$ go get gopkg.in/mgo.v2/bson
$ go get github.com/gorilla/mux
```

2. Create `read-record-mongodb.go`. Then we connect to the MongoDB database, read all the documents from an employee collection, marshal the list to JSON, and write it to an HTTP response stream, as follows:

```go
package main
import
(
  "encoding/json"
  "log"
  "net/http"
  "github.com/gorilla/mux"
  mgo "gopkg.in/mgo.v2"
  "gopkg.in/mgo.v2/bson"
)
const
(
  CONN_HOST = "localhost"
  CONN_PORT = "8080"
  MONGO_DB_URL = "127.0.0.1"
)
var session *mgo.Session
var connectionError error
func init()
{
  session, connectionError = mgo.Dial(MONGO_DB_URL)
  if connectionError != nil
  {
    log.Fatal("error connecting to database :: ", connectionError)
  }
  session.SetMode(mgo.Monotonic, true)
}
type Employee struct
{
  Id int `json:"uid"`
  Name string `json:"name"`
}
func readDocuments(w http.ResponseWriter, r *http.Request)
```

```
{
  log.Print("reading documents from database")
  var employees []Employee
  collection := session.DB("mydb").C("employee")
  err := collection.Find(bson.M{}).All(&employees)
  if err != nil
  {
    log.Print("error occurred while reading documents from
    database :: ", err)
    return
  }
  json.NewEncoder(w).Encode(employees)
}
func main()
{
  router := mux.NewRouter()
  router.HandleFunc("/employees", readDocuments).Methods("GET")
  defer session.Close()
  err := http.ListenAndServe(CONN_HOST+":"+CONN_PORT, router)
  if err != nil
  {
    log.Fatal("error starting http server :: ", err)
    return
  }
}
```

3. Run the program with the following command:

```
$ go run read-record-mongodb.go
```

How it works...

Once we run the program, the HTTP server will start locally listening on port 8080.

Next, browsing to `http://localhost:8080/employees` will give you the list of all employees from the MongoDB employee collection:

```
←  →  C  ⌂  ⓘ localhost:8080/employees

[{"uid":1,"name":"foo"}]
```

Let's look at the changes we introduced in the program:

1. Using `import ( "encoding/json" "log" "net/http" "github.com/gorilla/mux" mgo "gopkg.in/mgo.v2" "gopkg.in/mgo.v2/bson")`, we imported an additional `gopkg.in/mgo.v2/bson` package, which is a BSON specification for Go, and the `encoding/json` package, which we used to marshal the object list, which we got from MongoDB, to JSON.

2. Next, we defined a `readDocuments` handler, where we first get the employee collection from MongoDB, query for all the documents inside it, iterate over the documents to map it to an array of the `Employee` struct, and, finally, marshal it to JSON.

Updating your first document in MongoDB

Once a BSON document is created we may need to update some of its fields. In that case, we have to execute `update/upsert` queries on the MongoDB collection, which we will be covering in this recipe.

How to do it...

1. Install the `gopkg.in/mgo.v2`, `gopkg.in/mgo.v2/bson`, and `github.com/gorilla/mux` packages, using the `go get` command, as follows:

```
$ go get gopkg.in/mgo.v2
$ go get gopkg.in/mgo.v2/bson
$ go get github.com/gorilla/mux
```

2. Create `update-record-mongodb.go`. Then we connect to the MongoDB database, update the name of an employee for an ID, and write the number of records updated in MongoDB to an HTTP response stream, as follows:

```
package main
import
(
  "fmt"
  "log"
  "net/http"
  "strconv"
  "github.com/gorilla/mux"
```

```go
    mgo "gopkg.in/mgo.v2"
    "gopkg.in/mgo.v2/bson"
)
const
(
  CONN_HOST = "localhost"
  CONN_PORT = "8080"
  MONGO_DB_URL = "127.0.0.1"
)
var session *mgo.Session
var connectionError error
type Employee struct
{
  Id int `json:"uid"`
  Name string `json:"name"`
}
func init()
{
  session, connectionError = mgo.Dial(MONGO_DB_URL)
  if connectionError != nil
  {
    log.Fatal("error connecting to database :: ",
    connectionError)
  }
  session.SetMode(mgo.Monotonic, true)
}
func updateDocument(w http.ResponseWriter, r *http.Request)
{
  vars := mux.Vars(r)
  id := vars["id"]
  vals := r.URL.Query()
  name, ok := vals["name"]
  if ok
  {
    employeeId, err := strconv.Atoi(id)
    if err != nil
    {
      log.Print("error converting string id to int :: ", err)
      return
    }
    log.Print("going to update document in database
    for id :: ", id)
    collection := session.DB("mydb").C("employee")
    var changeInfo *mgo.ChangeInfo
    changeInfo, err = collection.Upsert(bson.M{"id": employeeId},
    &Employee{employeeId, name[0]})
    if err != nil
    {
```

```
                    log.Print("error occurred while updating record in
                    database :: ", err)
                    return
                }
                fmt.Fprintf(w, "Number of documents updated in database
                are :: %d", changeInfo.Updated)
            }
            else
            {
                fmt.Fprintf(w, "Error occurred while updating document
                in database for id :: %s", id)
            }
}
func main()
{
    router := mux.NewRouter()
    router.HandleFunc("/employee/update/{id}",
    updateDocument).Methods("PUT")
    defer session.Close()
    err := http.ListenAndServe(CONN_HOST+":"+CONN_PORT, router)
    if err != nil
    {
        log.Fatal("error starting http server :: ", err)
        return
    }
}
```

3. Run the program with the following command:

```
$ go run update-record-mongodb.go
```

How it works...

Once we run the program, the HTTP server will start locally listening on port 8080.

Next, executing a PUT request to UPDATE an employee document from the command line as follows will give you the number of documents updated in MongoDB:

```
$ curl -X PUT http://localhost:8080/employee/update/1\?name\=bar
Number of documents updated in database are :: 1
```

Let's look at the program we have written:

1. We defined an `updateDocument` handler, which gets the ID to be updated in MongoDB as a URL path variable and the new name as the HTTP request variable. As request variables are of string type, we have converted the variable ID of `string` type to `int` type. Then, we get the employee collection from MongoDB and call the `collection.Upsert` handler to insert if not present, or update an employee document with a new name for the supplied ID.

2. Next, we registered an `updateDocument` handler to be called for the URL pattern `/employee/update/{id}` for every `PUT` request with `gorilla/mux` router and close the MongoDB session, using the `defer session.Close()` statement once we return from the `main()` function.

Deleting your first document from MongoDB

Whenever we want to clean up the database or delete the documents that are no longer needed, we can easily remove them using a MongoDB driver for Go (`gopkg.in/mgo.v2`), which we will be covering in this recipe.

How to do it...

1. Install the `gopkg.in/mgo.v2`, `gopkg.in/mgo.v2/bson`, and `github.com/gorilla/mux` packages, using the `go get` command, as follows:

```
$ go get gopkg.in/mgo.v2
$ go get gopkg.in/mgo.v2/bson
$ go get github.com/gorilla/mux
```

2. Create `delete-record-mongodb.go`. Then we connect to MongoDB, get the name of an employee to be deleted from the database as an HTTP request variable, get the named collection, and remove the document, as follows:

```
package main
import
(
  "fmt"
  "log"
  "net/http"
  "github.com/gorilla/mux"
  mgo "gopkg.in/mgo.v2"
```

```
    "gopkg.in/mgo.v2/bson"
)
const
(
  CONN_HOST = "localhost"
  CONN_PORT = "8080"
  MONGO_DB_URL = "127.0.0.1"
)
var session *mgo.Session
var connectionError error
type Employee struct
{
  Id int `json:"uid"`
  Name string `json:"name"`
}
func init()
{
  session, connectionError = mgo.Dial(MONGO_DB_URL)
  if connectionError != nil
  {
    log.Fatal("error connecting to database :: ",
    connectionError)
  }
  session.SetMode(mgo.Monotonic, true)
}
func deleteDocument(w http.ResponseWriter, r *http.Request)
{
  vals := r.URL.Query()
  name, ok := vals["name"]
  if ok
  {
    log.Print("going to delete document in database for
    name :: ", name[0])
    collection := session.DB("mydb").C("employee")
    removeErr := collection.Remove(bson.M{"name": name[0]})
    if removeErr != nil
    {
      log.Print("error removing document from
      database :: ", removeErr)
      return
    }
    fmt.Fprintf(w, "Document with name %s is deleted from
    database", name[0])
  }
  else
  {
    fmt.Fprintf(w, "Error occurred while deleting document
    in database for name :: %s", name[0])
```

```
    }
  }
  func main()
  {
    router := mux.NewRouter()
    router.HandleFunc("/employee/delete",
    deleteDocument).Methods("DELETE")
    defer session.Close()
    err := http.ListenAndServe(CONN_HOST+":"+CONN_PORT, router)
    if err != nil
    {
      log.Fatal("error starting http server :: ", err)
      return
    }
  }
```

3. Run the program with the following command:

```
$ go run delete-record-mongodb.go
```

How it works...

Once we run the program, the HTTP server will start locally listening on port 8080.

Next, executing a DELETE request to delete a BSON document from the command line as follows will give you the name of the document deleted from the database:

```
$ curl -X DELETE http://localhost:8080/employee/delete?name\=bar
Document with name bar is deleted from database
```

Let's look at the program we have written:

1. We defined a deleteDocument handler, which gets the name to be deleted from MongoDB as the request variable, gets the employee collection from MongoDB, and calls the collection.Remove handler to remove a document for a given name.

2. Then, we registered a deleteDocument handler to be called for the URL pattern /employee/delete for every DELETE request with a gorilla/mux router, and closed the MongoDB session, using the defer session.Close() statement once we returned from the main() function.

6
Writing Microservices in Go Using Micro – a Microservice Toolkit

In this chapter, we will cover the following recipes:

- Creating your first protocol buffer
- Spinning up a microservice discovery client
- Creating your first microservice
- Creating your second microservice
- Creating your Micro API
- Interacting with microservices using a command-line interface and web UI

Introduction

With organizations now moving toward DevOps, microservices have started gaining popularity as well. As these services are independent in nature and can be developed in any language it allows organizations to focus on their development. With knowledge of the concepts covered in this chapter, we will be able to write microservices using Go Micro in a fairly easy way.

In this chapter, we will start by writing the protocol buffer. Then we will learn how we can spin up Consul, which is a Microservice discovery client, and eventually move on to create microservices and interact with them through the command line and web dashboard.

Creating your first protocol buffer

Protocol buffers are a flexible, efficient, and automated mechanism for encoding and serializing structured data supported by Go. In this recipe, we will learn how to write our first protocol buffer.

Getting ready...

1. Verify whether `protoc` is installed by executing the following command:

   ```
   $ protoc --version
     libprotoc 3.3.2
   ```

2. Install `protobuf` by way of the following:

   ```
   $ git clone https://github.com/google/protobuf
   $ cd protobuf
   $ ./autogen.sh
   $ ./configure
   $ make
   $ make check
   $ make install
   ```

How to do it...

1. Create `hello.proto` inside the `proto` directory and define a `service` interface with the name `Say`, which has two datatypes—`Request` and `Response`, as follows:

   ```
   syntax = "proto3";
   service Say
   {
     rpc Hello(Request) returns (Response) {}
   }
   message Request
   {
     string name = 1;
   }
   message Response
   {
     string msg = 1;
   }
   ```

2. Compile `hello.proto` with the following command:

```
$ protoc --go_out=plugins=micro:. hello.proto
```

How it works...

Once the command has executed successfully, `hello.pb.go` will be created inside the `proto` directory, which will look like as shown in the following screenshot:

Let's understand the `.proto` file we have written:

- `syntax = "proto3";`: Here we specify that we are using `proto3` syntax, which makes the compiler understand that the protocol buffer has to be compiled with version 3. If we don't specify the syntax explicitly then the compiler assumes we are using `proto2`.
- `service Say { rpc Hello(Request) returns (Response) {} }`: Here we defined an RPC service with the name `Say` and a `Hello` method that takes `Request` and returns a `Response`.
- `message Request { string name = 1; }`: Here we defined the `Request` data type that has a `name` field.
- `message Response { string msg = 1; }`: Here we defined the `Response` data type that has a `msg` field.

Spinning up a microservice discovery client

In a microservices architecture where multiple services are deployed, the service discovery client helps the application to find out the services they are dependent on, which can be either through DNS or HTTP. When we talk about service discovery clients one of the most common and famous is `Consul` by HashiCorp, which we will be spinning up in this recipe.

Getting ready...

Verify whether `Consul` is installed by executing the following command:

```
$ consul version
 Consul v0.8.5
 Protocol 2 spoken by default, understands 2 to 3 (agent will automatically
use protocol >2 when speaking to compatible agents)
```

How to do it...

Start `consul agent` in server mode by executing the following command:

```
$ consul agent -dev
```

How it works...

Once the command has executed successfully the Consul agent starts running in server mode, giving us the following output:

```
==> Starting Consul agent...
==> Consul agent running!
           Version: 'v0.8.5'
           Node ID: 'ba19a892-7e82-ba57-8d2c-dc41cf826256'
         Node name: 'apples-MacBook-Pro-3.local'
        Datacenter: 'dc1'
            Server: true (bootstrap: false)
       Client Addr: 127.0.0.1 (HTTP: 8500, HTTPS: -1, DNS: 8600)
      Cluster Addr: 127.0.0.1 (LAN: 8301, WAN: 8302)
     Gossip encrypt: false, RPC-TLS: false, TLS-Incoming: false

==> Log data will now stream in as it occurs:

    2018/04/04 23:54:24 [DEBUG] Using random ID "ba19a892-7e82-ba57-8d2c-dc41cf826256" as node ID
    2018/04/04 23:54:24 [INFO] raft: Initial configuration (index=1): [{Suffrage:Voter ID:127.0.0.1:8300 Address:127.0.0.1:8300}]
    2018/04/04 23:54:24 [INFO] raft: Node at 127.0.0.1:8300 [Follower] entering Follower state (Leader: "")
    2018/04/04 23:54:24 [INFO] serf: EventMemberJoin: apples-MacBook-Pro-3.local 127.0.0.1
    2018/04/04 23:54:24 [INFO] consul: Adding LAN server apples-MacBook-Pro-3.local (Addr: tcp/127.0.0.1:8300) (DC: dc1)
    2018/04/04 23:54:24 [INFO] serf: EventMemberJoin: apples-MacBook-Pro-3.local.dc1 127.0.0.1
    2018/04/04 23:54:24 [INFO] consul: Handled member-join event for server "apples-MacBook-Pro-3.local.dc1" in area "wan"
    2018/04/04 23:54:24 [INFO] agent: Started DNS server 127.0.0.1:8600 (udp)
    2018/04/04 23:54:24 [INFO] agent: Started DNS server 127.0.0.1:8600 (tcp)
    2018/04/04 23:54:24 [INFO] agent: Started HTTP server on 127.0.0.1:8500
    2018/04/04 23:54:24 [WARN] raft: Heartbeat timeout from "" reached, starting election
    2018/04/04 23:54:24 [INFO] raft: Node at 127.0.0.1:8300 [Candidate] entering Candidate state in term 2
    2018/04/04 23:54:24 [DEBUG] raft: Votes needed: 1
    2018/04/04 23:54:24 [DEBUG] raft: Vote granted from 127.0.0.1:8300 in term 2. Tally: 1
    2018/04/04 23:54:24 [INFO] raft: Election won. Tally: 1
    2018/04/04 23:54:24 [INFO] raft: Node at 127.0.0.1:8300 [Leader] entering Leader state
    2018/04/04 23:54:24 [INFO] consul: cluster leadership acquired
    2018/04/04 23:54:24 [INFO] consul: New leader elected: apples-MacBook-Pro-3.local
    2018/04/04 23:54:24 [DEBUG] consul: reset tombstone GC to index 3
    2018/04/04 23:54:24 [INFO] consul: member 'apples-MacBook-Pro-3.local' joined, marking health alive
    2018/04/04 23:54:24 [INFO] agent: Synced service 'consul'
    2018/04/04 23:54:24 [DEBUG] agent: Node info in sync
```

We can also list the members of the Consul cluster by executing the following command:

```
$ consul members
```

This will give us the following result:

```
→ ~ consul members
Node                        Address            Status  Type    Build  Protocol  DC
apples-MacBook-Pro-3.local  127.0.0.1:8301     alive   server  0.8.5  2         dc1
→ ~
```

 Because Consul can be run either in server or client mode with at least one server, to keep the setup at a bare minimum we have started our agent in server mode, though it is not recommended because there are chances of data loss in a failure scenario.

Moreover, browsing to `http://localhost:8500/ui/` will display the Consul web UI where we can view all the services and nodes, as follows:

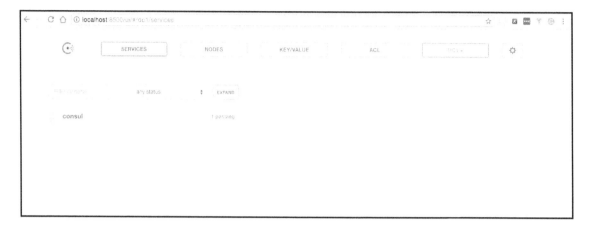

Creating your first microservice

A microservice is just a piece of code that runs as a unique process and communicates through a well-defined, lightweight mechanism to serve a business goal, which we will be writing in this recipe using `https://github.com/micro/micro` though there are a number of libraries available such as `https://github.com/go-kit/kit` and `https://github.com/grpc/grpc-go`, which serve the same purpose.

Getting ready...

1. Start `consul agent` by executing the following command:

   ```
   $ consul agent -dev
   ```

2. Install and run `micro` by executing the following commands:

   ```
   $ go get github.com/micro/micro
   $ micro api
    2018/02/06 00:03:36 Registering RPC Handler at /rpc
    2018/02/06 00:03:36 Registering API Default Handler at /
    2018/02/06 00:03:36 Listening on [::]:8080
    2018/02/06 00:03:36 Listening on [::]:54814
   ```

```
2018/02/06 00:03:36 Broker Listening on [::]:54815
2018/02/06 00:03:36 Registering node: go.micro.api-
a6a82a54-0aaf-11e8-8d64-685b35d52676
```

How to do it...

1. Create `first-greeting-service.go` inside the `services` directory by executing the command $ `mkdir services && cd services && touch first-greeting-service.go`.

2. Copy the following content to `first-greeting-service.go`:

```
package main
import
(
  "log"
  "time"
  hello "../proto"
  "github.com/micro/go-micro"
)
type Say struct{}
func (s *Say) Hello(ctx context.Context, req *hello.Request,
rsp *hello.Response) error
{
  log.Print("Received Say.Hello request - first greeting service")
  rsp.Msg = "Hello " + req.Name
  return nil
}
func main()
{
  service := micro.NewService
  (
    micro.Name("go.micro.service.greeter"),
    micro.RegisterTTL(time.Second*30),
    micro.RegisterInterval(time.Second*10),
  )
  service.Init()
  hello.RegisterSayHandler(service.Server(), new(Say))
  if err := service.Run(); err != nil
  {
    log.Fatal("error starting service : ", err)
    return
  }
}
```

With everything in place, the directory structure should look like the following:

3. Move to the `services` directory and run the program with the following command:

```
$ go run first-greeting-service.go
```

How it works...

Once we run the program, the RPC server will start locally listening on port `8080`.

Next, execute a `POST` request from the command line as follows:

```
$ curl -X POST -H 'Content-Type: application/json' -d '{"service":
"go.micro.service.greeter", "method": "Say.Hello", "request": {"name":
"Arpit Aggarwal"}}' http://localhost:8080/rpc
```

This will give us **Hello** followed by the name as a response from the server as shown in the following screenshot:

```
    curl -X POST -H 'Content-Type: application/json' -d '{"service": "go.micro.service.greeter", "method": "Say.Hello", "request": {"name": "Arpit Aggarwal"}}' http://localhost:808
0/rpc
{"msg":"Hello Arpit Aggarwal"}
    {"msg":"Hello Arpit Aggarwal"}
```

Looking at the logs of the `first-greeting-service.go` will show us that the request is served by the first greeting service, as follows:

```
    services git:(master) go run first-greeting-service.go
2018/04/08 19:12:23 Listening on [::]:60667
2018/04/08 19:12:23 Broker Listening on [::]:60668
2018/04/08 19:12:23 Registering node: go.micro.service.greeter-aa9eeecc-3b32-11e8-8132-685b35d52676
2018/04/08 19:12:28 Received Say.Hello request - first greeting service
```

Let's look at the program we have written:

- Using `import ("log" "time" hello "../proto"` `"github.com/micro/go-micro" "golang.org/x/net/context")`, we imported `"hello "../proto"`, a directory that includes protocol buffer source code and compiled protocol buffer suffixed `.pb.go`. Additionally, we imported the `github.com/micro/go-micro` package, which consists of all the libraries required to write the microservice.

- Next, we defined a `main()` handler where we create a new service with the name `go.micro.service.greeter` using `micro.NewService()`, initialize it, register the handler with it, and finally start it.

Creating your second microservice

In this recipe, we will create another microservice using `go-micro`, which is a replica of the `first-greeting-service.go` except for the logger message printed on the console that demonstrates the concept of client-side load balancing between the two different instances of a service with the same name.

How to do it...

1. Create `second-greeting-service.go` inside the `services` directory by executing the command `$ cd services && touch second-greeting-service.go`.

2. Copy the following content to `second-greeting-service.go`:

```
package main
import
(
  "context"
  "log"
  "time"
  hello "../proto"
  "github.com/micro/go-micro"
)
type Say struct{}
func (s *Say) Hello(ctx context.Context, req *hello.Request,
rsp *hello.Response) error
{
```

```
log.Print("Received Say.Hello request - second greeting
service")
rsp.Msg = "Hello " + req.Name
return nil
}
func main()
{
  service := micro.NewService
  (
    micro.Name("go.micro.service.greeter"),
    micro.RegisterTTL(time.Second*30),
    micro.RegisterInterval(time.Second*10),
  )
  service.Init()
  hello.RegisterSayHandler(service.Server(), new(Say))
  if err := service.Run(); err != nil
  {
    log.Fatal("error starting service : ", err)
    return
  }
}
```

With everything in place, the directory structure should look like the following:

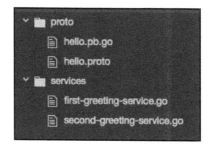

3. Move to the `services` directory and run the program with the following command:

```
$ go run second-greeting-service.go
```

How it works...

Once we run the program, the RPC server will start locally listening on port `8080`.

Next, execute a `POST` request from the command line as follows:

```
$ curl -X POST -H 'Content-Type: application/json' -d '{"service":
"go.micro.service.greeter", "method": "Say.Hello", "request": {"name":
"Arpit Aggarwal"}}' http://localhost:8080/rpc
```

This will give us **Hello** followed by the name as a response from the server, as follows:

```
~ curl -X POST -H 'Content-Type: application/json' -d '{"service": "go.micro.service.greeter", "method": "Say.Hello", "request": {"name": "Arpit Aggarwal"}}' http://localhost:808
0/rpc
{"msg":"Hello Arpit Aggarwal"}
```

Looking at the logs of the `second-greeting-service.go` will show us the request is served by the second greeting service:

```
~ services git:(master) go run second-greeting-service.go
2018/04/08 19:24:30 Listening on [::]:61505
2018/04/08 19:24:30 Broker Listening on [::]:61506
2018/04/08 19:24:30 Registering node: go.micro.service.greeter-5bf9291d-3b34-11e8-9179-685b35d52676
2018/04/08 19:24:35 Received Say.Hello request - second greeting service
```

Now, if we execute a `POST` request again then it will print the logs in the `first-greeting-service.go` console, which is because of the smart, client-side, load balancing of services built on discovery offered by Go Micro:

```
~ services git:(master) go run first-greeting-service.go
2018/04/08 19:12:23 Listening on [::]:60667
2018/04/08 19:12:23 Broker Listening on [::]:60668
2018/04/08 19:12:23 Registering node: go.micro.service.greeter-aa9eeecc-3b32-11e8-8132-685b35d52676
2018/04/08 19:12:28 Received Say.Hello request - first greeting service
2018/04/08 19:25:10 Received Say.Hello request - first greeting service
```

Creating your Micro API

So far, we have explicitly called a backend service by name and a method to access it. In this recipe, we will learn how we can access the services using Go Micro API, which implements an API gateway pattern to provide a single entry point to the microservices. The advantage of using Go Micro API is that it serves over HTTP and dynamically routes to the appropriate backend service using HTTP handlers.

Getting ready...

Start `consul agent`, `micro API`, `first-greeting-service.go`, and `second-greeting-service.go` in separate terminals by executing the following commands:

```
$ consul agent -dev
$ micro api
$ go run first-greeting-service.go
$ go run second-greeting-service.go
```

How to do it...

1. Create `greeting-api.go` inside the `api` directory by executing the command `$ mkdir api && cd api && touch greeting-api.go`.

2. Copy the following content to `greeting-api.go`:

```
package main
import
(
  "context"
  "encoding/json"
  "log"
  "strings"
  hello "../proto"
  "github.com/micro/go-micro"
  api "github.com/micro/micro/api/proto"
)
type Say struct
{
  Client hello.SayClient
}
func (s *Say) Hello(ctx context.Context, req *api.Request,
rsp *api.Response) error
{
  log.Print("Received Say.Hello request - Micro Greeter API")
  name, ok := req.Get["name"]
  if ok
  {
    response, err := s.Client.Hello
    (
      ctx, &hello.Request
      {
        Name: strings.Join(name.Values, " "),
      }
```

```
  )
  if err != nil
  {
    return err
  }
  message, _ := json.Marshal
  (
    map[string]string
    {
      "message": response.Msg,
    }
  )
  rsp.Body = string(message)
  }
  return nil
}
func main()
{
  service := micro.NewService
  (
    micro.Name("go.micro.api.greeter"),
  )
  service.Init()
  service.Server().Handle
  (
    service.Server().NewHandler
    (
      &Say{Client: hello.NewSayClient("go.micro.service.
      greeter", service.Client())},
    ),
  )
  if err := service.Run(); err != nil
  {
    log.Fatal("error starting micro api : ", err)
    return
  }
}
```

With everything in place, the directory structure should look like the following:

3. Move to the `api` directory and run the program with the following command:

```
$ go run greeting-api.go
```

How it works...

Once we run the program, the HTTP server will start locally listening on port 8080.

Next, browse to `http://localhost:8080/greeter/say/hello?name=Arpit+Aggarwal` as follows:

```
←    C  ⌂  ⓘ localhost:8080/greeter/say/hello?name=Arpit+Aggarwal

{"message":"Hello Arpit Aggarwal"}
```

This will give you the response **Hello** followed by the name received as an HTTP request variable. Moreover, looking at the logs of the `second-greeting-service.go` will show us the request is served by the second greeting service, as follows:

```
→  services git:(master) go run second-greeting-service.go
2018/04/08 19:24:30 Listening on [::]:61505
2018/04/08 19:24:30 Broker Listening on [::]:61506
2018/04/08 19:24:30 Registering node: go.micro.service.greeter-5bf9291d-3b34-11e8-9179-685b35d52676
2018/04/08 19:24:35 Received Say.Hello request - second greeting service
```

Now, if we execute a GET request again then it will print the logs in the first-greeting-service.go console, which is because of the smart, client-side, load balancing of services built on discovery offered by Go Micro:

```
→  services git:(master) go run first-greeting-service.go
2018/04/08 19:12:23 Listening on [::]:60667
2018/04/08 19:12:23 Broker Listening on [::]:60668
2018/04/08 19:12:23 Registering node: go.micro.service.greeter-aa9eeecc-3b32-11e8-8132-685b35d52676
2018/04/08 19:12:28 Received Say.Hello request - first greeting service
2018/04/08 19:25:10 Received Say.Hello request - first greeting service
```

Interacting with microservices using a command-line interface and web UI

So far, we have used the command line to execute GET and POST HTTP requests to access services. This can also be achieved by way of the Go Micro web user interface as well. All we need to do is start micro web, which we will be covering in this recipe.

How to do it...

1. Install the go get github.com/micro/micro package using the go get command, as follows:

   ```
   $ go get github.com/micro/micro
   ```

2. Run the web UI with the following command:

   ```
   $ micro web
   ```

How it works...

Once a command has executed successfully, browsing to `http://localhost:8082/registry` will list all the registered services as shown in the following screenshot:

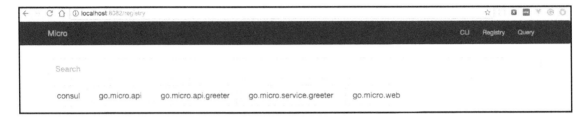

Querying our `greeter` service using the web UI with the request `{"name" : "Arpit Aggarwal"}` will render you the response, `{"msg": "Hello Arpit Aggarwal"}` :

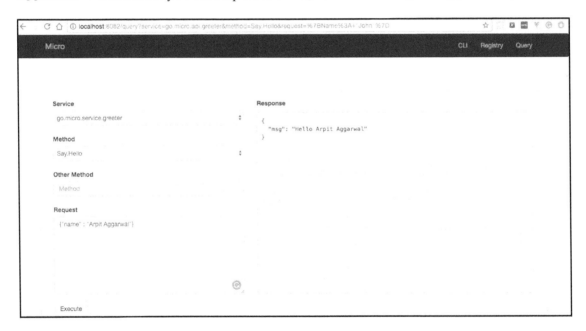

Querying the same `greeter` service using a `CLI` command, `query`
`go.micro.service.greeter Say.Hello {"name" : "Arpit Aggarwal"}` will render
you the response, `{"msg": "Hello Arpit Aggarwal"}`:

Working with WebSocket in Go

7

In this chapter, we will cover the following recipes:

- Creating your first WebSocket server
- Creating your first WebSocket client
- Debugging your first local WebSocket server
- Debugging your first remote WebSocket server
- Unit testing your first WebSocket server

Introduction

WebSocket provides a bidirectional, single-socket, full-duplex connection between the server and the client, making real-time communication much more efficient than other ways such as long polling and server-sent events.

With WebSocket, the client and the server can talk independently, each able to send and receive information at the same time after the initial handshake, reusing the same connection from the client to the server and the server to the client, which eventually reduces the delay and server load greatly, allowing web applications to perform modern tasks in the most effective way. The WebSocket protocol is supported by most major browsers, including Google Chrome, Microsoft Edge, Internet Explorer, Firefox, Safari, and Opera. So there are no compatibility issues.

In this chapter, we will learn how to create a WebSocket server and client, writing unit tests and debugging the server running either locally or remotely.

Creating your first WebSocket server

In this recipe, we will learn how to write a WebSocket server, which is a TCP application listening on port 8080 that allows connected clients to send messages to each other.

How to do it...

1. Install the `github.com/gorilla/websocket` package using the `go get` command, as follows:

   ```
   $ go get github.com/gorilla/websocket
   ```

2. Create `websocket-server.go` where we will upgrade an HTTP request to WebSocket, read the JSON message from the client, and broadcast it to all of the connected clients, as follows:

   ```go
   package main
   import
   (
     "log"
     "net/http"
     "github.com/gorilla/websocket"
   )
   var clients = make(map[*websocket.Conn]bool)
   var broadcast = make(chan Message)
   var upgrader = websocket.Upgrader{}
   type Message struct
   {
     Message string `json:"message"`
   }
   func HandleClients(w http.ResponseWriter, r *http.Request)
   {
     go broadcastMessagesToClients()
     websocket, err := upgrader.Upgrade(w, r, nil)
     if err != nil
     {
       log.Fatal("error upgrading GET request to a
       websocket :: ", err)
     }
     defer websocket.Close()
     clients[websocket] = true
     for
     {
       var message Message
   ```

```go
    err := websocket.ReadJSON(&message)
    if err != nil
    {
      log.Printf("error occurred while reading
      message : %v", err)
      delete(clients, websocket)
      break
    }
    broadcast <- message
  }
}
func main()
{
  http.HandleFunc
  (
    "/", func(w http.ResponseWriter,
    r *http.Request)
    {
      http.ServeFile(w, r, "index.html")
    }
  )
  http.HandleFunc("/echo", HandleClients)
  err := http.ListenAndServe(":8080", nil)
  if err != nil
  {
    log.Fatal("error starting http server :: ", err)
    return
  }
}
func broadcastMessagesToClients()
{
  for
  {
    message := <-broadcast
    for client := range clients
    {
      err := client.WriteJSON(message)
      if err != nil
      {
        log.Printf("error occurred while writing
        message to client: %v", err)
        client.Close()
        delete(clients, client)
      }
    }
  }
}
```

3. Run the program with the following command:

```
$ go run websocket-server.go
```

How it works...

Once we run the program, the WebSocket server will start locally listening on port `8080`.

Let's understand the program we have written:

1. We used `import ("log" "net/http" "github.com/gorilla/websocket")` which is a preprocessor command that tells the Go compiler to include all files from the `log`, `net/http`, and `github.com/gorilla/websocket` packages.
2. Using `var clients = make(map[*websocket.Conn]bool)`, we created a map that represents the clients connected to a WebSocket server with KeyType as a WebSocket connection object and ValueType as Boolean.
3. Using `var broadcast = make(chan Message)`, we created a channel where all the received messages are written.
4. Next, we defined a `HandleClients` handler, which upon receiving the `HTTP GET` request, upgrades it to `WebSocket`, registers the client with the socket server, reads the requested JSON messages, and writes it to the broadcast channel.
5. Then, we defined a Go function `broadcastMessagesToClients`, which grabs the messages written to the broadcast channel and sends it out to every client that is currently connected to the WebSocket server.

Creating your first WebSocket client

In this recipe, we will create a simple client to start the WebSocket handshake process. The client will send a pretty standard `HTTP GET` request to the WebSocket server and the server upgrades it through an Upgrade header in the response.

How to do it...

1. Create `index.html` where we will open a connection to a non-secure WebSocket server on page load, as follows:

```html
<html>
  <title>WebSocket Server</title>
  <input id="input" type="text" />
  <button onclick="send()">Send</button>
  <pre id="output"></pre>
  <script>
    var input = document.getElementById("input");
    var output = document.getElementById("output");
    var socket = new WebSocket("ws://" + window.
    location.host + "/echo");
    socket.onopen = function ()
    {
      output.innerHTML += "Status: Connected\n";
    };
    socket.onmessage = function (e)
    {
      output.innerHTML += "Message from Server: " +
      e.data + "\n";
    };
    function send()
    {
      socket.send
      (
        JSON.stringify
        (
          {
            message: input.value
          }
        )
      );
      input.value = "";
    }
  </script>
</html>
```

With everything in place, the directory structure should look like the following:

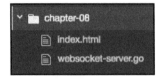

2. Run the program with the following command:

```
$ go run websocket-server.go
```

How it works...

Once we run the program, the WebSocket server will start locally listening on port 8080.

Browsing to http://localhost:8080 will show us the WebSocket client page with a textbox and a **Send** button as shown in the following screenshot:

Debugging your first local WebSocket server

Debugging a web application is one of the most important skills for a developer to learn, as it helps in identifying a problem, isolating the source of the problem, and then either correcting the problem or determining a way to work around it. In this recipe, we will learn how to debug a WebSocket server running locally using GoLand IDE.

Getting ready...

This recipe assumes you have GoLand IDE installed and configured to run the Go Application on your machine.

How to do it...

1. Click **Open Project** in the GoLand IDE to open `websocket-server.go`, which we wrote in our previous recipe, as shown in the following screenshot:

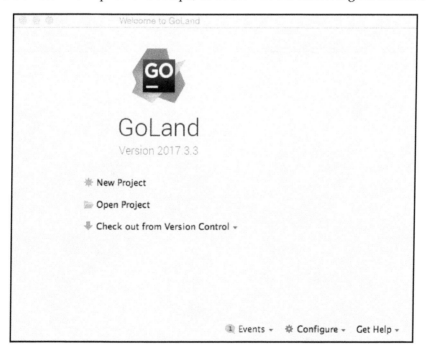

2. Once the project opens, click on **Edit Configurations** as shown in the following screenshot:

3. Select **Add New Configuration** by clicking the + sign as shown in the following screenshot:

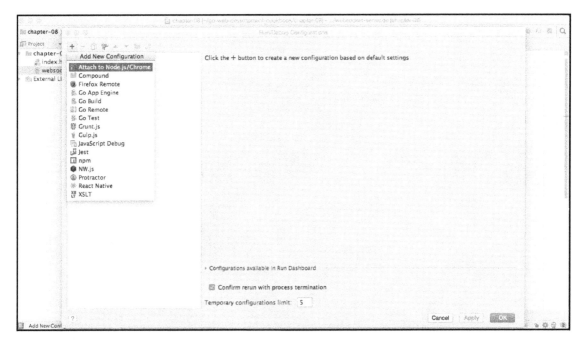

4. Select **Go Build**, rename the configuration to `WebSocket Local Debug`, change **Run kind** to **Directory**, and click on **Apply** and **OK** as shown in the following screenshot:

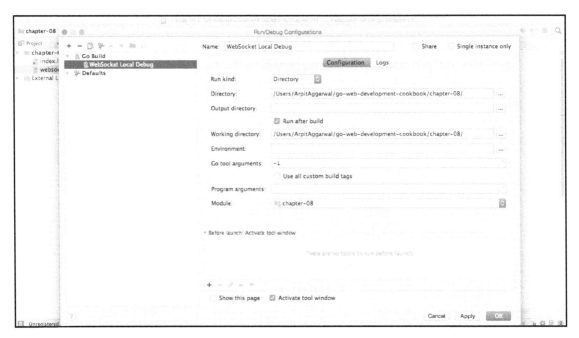

5. Place a few breakpoints and click on the **Debug** button:

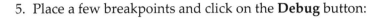

```
package main

import ...

var clients = make(map[*websocket.Conn]bool)
var broadcast = make(chan Message)

var upgrader = websocket.Upgrader{}

type Message struct {
    Message string `json:"message"`
}

func HandleClients(w http.ResponseWriter, r *http.Request) {
    go broadcastMessagesToClients()

    websocket, err := upgrader.Upgrade(w, r, responseHeader: nil)
    if err != nil {
        log.Fatal( v "error upgrading GET request to a websocket :: ", err)
    }

    defer websocket.Close()

    clients[websocket] = true

    for {
        var message Message
        err := websocket.ReadJSON(&message)
        if err != nil {
            log.Printf( format: "error occurred while reading message : %v", err)
            delete(clients, websocket)
            break
        }
        broadcast <- message
    }
}

func main() {
    http.HandleFunc( pattern: "/", func(w http.ResponseWriter, r *http.Request) {
        HandleClients(w http.ResponseWriter, r *http.Request)
```

How it works...

Once we run the program, the WebSocket server will start locally in debug mode listening on port `8080`.

Browsing to `http://localhost:8080` will show us the WebSocket client page with a textbox and a **Send** button as shown in the following screenshot:

Enter text and click on the **Send** button to see the program execution stopping at the breakpoints we placed in the GoLand IDE, as follows:

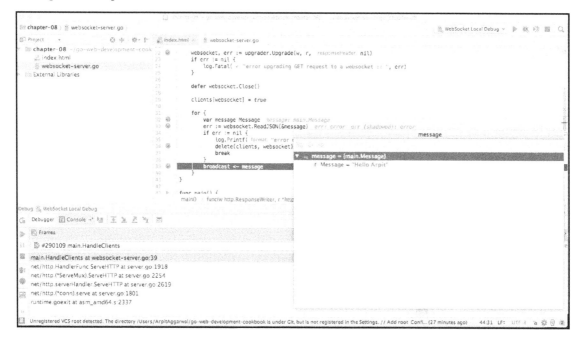

Debugging your first remote WebSocket server

In the previous recipe, we learnt how to debug a WebSocket server that is running locally. In this recipe, we will learn how to debug it if it is running on another or a remote machine.

The steps are more or less the same as we took in the previous recipe except for the debug configuration section where we will change the localhost to the remote machine IP or DNS and start the Delve server, which is a debugger for the Go programming language on the remote machine.

How to do it...

1. Add another configuration by clicking on **Edit Configurations...** as shown in the following screenshot:

2. Click on the + sign to **Add New Configuration** and select **Go Remote**:

3. Rename the debug configuration to `WebSocket Remote Debug`, change the **Host** to `remote-machine-IP` or `DNS`, and click on **Apply** and **OK** as shown in the following screenshot:

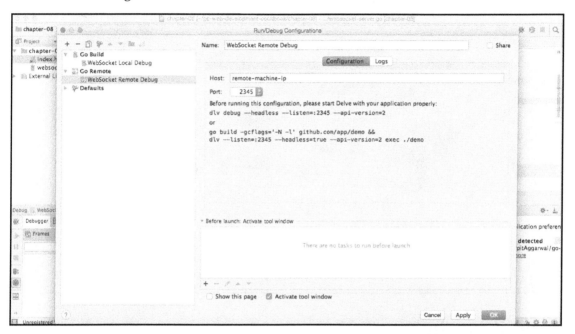

4. Run a headless Delve server on the target or remote machine by executing the following command:

```
dlv debug --headless --listen=:2345 --api-version=2
```

The preceding command will start an API server listening on port 2345.

5. Select **WebSocket Remote Debug** configuration and click on the **Debug** button:

How it works...

Browse to the remotely available WebSocket client page, enter some text, and click on the **Send** button to see the program execution stopping at the breakpoints we placed:

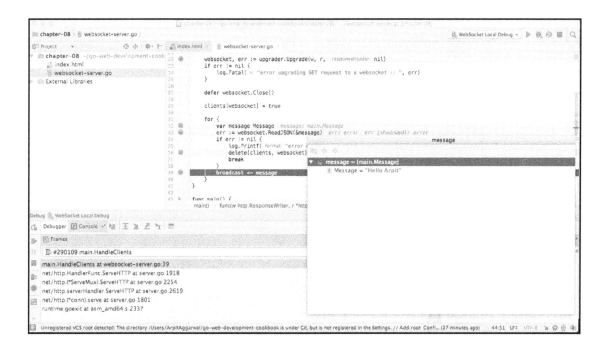

Unit testing your first WebSocket server

Unit testing or test-driven development helps the developer to design loosely-coupled code with the focus on code reusability. It also helps us to realize when to stop coding and make changes quickly.

In this recipe, we will learn how to write a unit test for the WebSocket server that we have already written in one of our previous recipes.

See the *Creating your first WebSocket server* recipe.

How to do it...

1. Install the `github.com/gorilla/websocket` and `github.com/stretchr/testify/assert` packages using the `go get` command, as follows:

```
$ go get github.com/gorilla/websocket
$ go get github.com/stretchr/testify/assert
```

2. Create `websocket-server_test.go` where we will create a test server, connect to it using the Gorilla client, and eventually read and write messages to test the connection, as follows:

```go
package main
import
(
  "net/http"
  "net/http/httptest"
  "strings"
  "testing"
  "github.com/gorilla/websocket"
  "github.com/stretchr/testify/assert"
)
func TestWebSocketServer(t *testing.T)
{
  server := httptest.NewServer(http.HandlerFunc
  (HandleClients))
  defer server.Close()
  u := "ws" + strings.TrimPrefix(server.URL, "http")
  socket, _, err := websocket.DefaultDialer.Dial(u, nil)
  if err != nil
  {
    t.Fatalf("%v", err)
  }
  defer socket.Close()
  m := Message{Message: "hello"}
  if err := socket.WriteJSON(&m); err != nil
  {
    t.Fatalf("%v", err)
  }
  var message Message
  err = socket.ReadJSON(&message)
  if err != nil
  {
    t.Fatalf("%v", err)
  }
```

```
                assert.Equal(t, "hello", message.Message, "they
                should be equal")
        }
```

How it works...

Execute a `go test` from the command line as follows:

```
$ go test websocket-server_test.go websocket-server.go
ok   command-line-arguments 0.048s
```

It will give us the response `ok`, which means the test compiled and executed successfully.

Let's see how it looks when a Go test fails. Change the expected output in the `assert` statement to something else. In the following `hello` has been changed to `hi`:

```
...
assert.Equal(t, "hi", message.Message, "they should be equal")
...
```

Execute the test again by running the `go test` command:

```
$ go test websocket-server_test.go websocket-server.go
```

It will give us the failure response along with the error trace as shown in the following screenshot:

```
--- FAIL: TestWebSocketServer (0.00s)
        websocket-server_test.go:36:
                        Error Trace:    websocket-server_test.go:36
                        Error:          Not equal:
                                        expected: "hi"
                                        actual  : "hello"
                        Test:           TestWebSocketServer
                        Messages:       they should be equal
FAIL
FAIL    command-line-arguments  0.138s
```

8
Working with the Go Web Application Framework – Beego

In this chapter, we will cover the following recipes:

- Creating your first project using Beego
- Creating your first controller and router
- Creating your first view
- Creating your first session variable
- Creating your first filter
- Handling HTTP errors in Beego
- Implementing caching in Beego
- Monitoring the Beego application
- Deploying the Beego application on a local machine
- Deploying the Beego application with Nginx

Introduction

A web application framework is a must whenever we are developing an application because it significantly speeds up and simplifies our work by eliminating the need to write a lot of repetitive code and providing features such as models, APIs, and other elements. Using an application framework, we can enjoy the perks of its architecture pattern and boost the development of an application.

A popular type of web application framework is **Model-View-Controller** (**MVC**) and there are many MVC frameworks available for Go, such as Revel, Utron, and Beego.

In this chapter, we will learn about Beego, which is one of the most popular and commonly used web MVC frameworks. We will start with creating the project and then move on to creating controllers, views, and filters. We will also look at implementing caching, and monitoring and deploying an application.

Creating your first project using Beego

The first and the foremost thing we have to do to start a project is to set up its basic architecture. In Beego, this can be achieved easily using a tool called bee, which we will cover in this recipe.

How to do it...

1. Install the github.com/beego/bee package using the go get command, as follows:

   ```
   $ go get github.com/beego/bee
   ```

2. Open a terminal to your $GOPATH/src directory and create a project using the bee new command, as follows:

   ```
   $ cd $GOPATH/src
   $ bee new my-first-beego-project
   ```

   Once the command has executed successfully, it will create a new Beego project, and the creation steps on the console will look like the following screenshot:

```
 src bee new my-first-beego-project

|     \
| |_/ /   ___    ___
|    \ / _ \ / _ \
| |_/ /|  __/| |__/
\____/  \___| \___|  v1.8.4
2018/04/03 16:05:23 INFO      ► 0001 Creating application...
        create  /Users/ArpitAggarwal/src/my-first-beego-project/
        create  /Users/ArpitAggarwal/src/my-first-beego-project/conf/
        create  /Users/ArpitAggarwal/src/my-first-beego-project/controllers/
        create  /Users/ArpitAggarwal/src/my-first-beego-project/models/
        create  /Users/ArpitAggarwal/src/my-first-beego-project/routers/
        create  /Users/ArpitAggarwal/src/my-first-beego-project/tests/
        create  /Users/ArpitAggarwal/src/my-first-beego-project/static/
        create  /Users/ArpitAggarwal/src/my-first-beego-project/static/js/
        create  /Users/ArpitAggarwal/src/my-first-beego-project/static/css/
        create  /Users/ArpitAggarwal/src/my-first-beego-project/static/img/
        create  /Users/ArpitAggarwal/src/my-first-beego-project/views/
        create  /Users/ArpitAggarwal/src/my-first-beego-project/conf/app.conf
        create  /Users/ArpitAggarwal/src/my-first-beego-project/controllers/default.go
        create  /Users/ArpitAggarwal/src/my-first-beego-project/views/index.tpl
        create  /Users/ArpitAggarwal/src/my-first-beego-project/routers/router.go
        create  /Users/ArpitAggarwal/src/my-first-beego-project/tests/default_test.go
        create  /Users/ArpitAggarwal/src/my-first-beego-project/main.go
2018/04/03 16:05:23 SUCCESS   ► 0002 New application successfully created!
```

3. Go to the path of the newly created project and enter bee run to compile and run the project, as follows:

```
$ cd $GOPATH/src/my-first-beego-project
$ bee run
```

Once, command has executed successfully, bee will build the project and start the application, as shown in the following screenshot:

```
→  my-first-beego-project bee run

|     \
| |_/ /   ___    ___
|    \ / _ \ / _ \
| |_/ /|  __/| |__/
\____/  \___| \___|  v1.8.4
2018/04/03 16:11:35 INFO      ► 0001 Using 'my-first-beego-project' as 'appname'
2018/04/03 16:11:35 INFO      ► 0002 Initializing watcher...
my-first-beego-project/controllers
my-first-beego-project/routers
my-first-beego-project
2018/04/03 16:11:56 SUCCESS   ► 0003 Built Successfully!
2018/04/03 16:11:56 INFO      ► 0004 Restarting 'my-first-beego-project'...
2018/04/03 16:11:56 SUCCESS   ► 0005 './my-first-beego-project' is running...
2018/04/03 16:11:56.778 [I] [asm_amd64.s:2337] http server Running on http://:8080
```

How it works...

Once the command has executed successfully, a web application will run on the default Beego port `8080` and browsing `http://localhost:8080/` will render the welcome page of the application, as shown in the following screenshot:

Creating your first controller and router

One of the main components of a web application is the controller, which acts as a coordinator between the view and the model and handles the user's requests, which could be a button click, or a menu selection, or HTTP `GET` and `POST` requests. In this recipe, we will learn how we can create a controller in Beego.

How to do it...

1. Move to `$GOPATH/src/my-first-beego-project/controllers` and create `firstcontroller.go`, as follows:

```
package controllers
import "github.com/astaxie/beego"
type FirstController struct
{
```

```
    beego.Controller
  }
  type Employee struct
  {
    Id int `json:"id"`
    FirstName string `json:"firstName"`
    LastName string `json:"lastName"`
  }
  type Employees []Employee
  var employees []Employee
  func init()
  {
    employees = Employees
    {
      Employee{Id: 1, FirstName: "Foo", LastName: "Bar"},
      Employee{Id: 2, FirstName: "Baz", LastName: "Qux"},
    }
  }
  func (this *FirstController) GetEmployees()
  {
    this.Ctx.ResponseWriter.WriteHeader(200)
    this.Data["json"] = employees
    this.ServeJSON()
  }
```

2. Move to $GOPATH/src/my-first-beego-project/routers and edit
   router.go to add GET mapping /employees, which will be handled by
   the GetEmployees handler defined in FirstController, as follows:

```
  package routers
  import
  (
    "my-first-beego-project/controllers"
    "github.com/astaxie/beego"
  )
  func init()
  {
    beego.Router("/", &controllers.MainController{})
    beego.Router("/employees", &controllers.FirstController{},
    "get:GetEmployees")
  }
```

3. Run the project using the following command:

```
  $ bee run
```

How it works...

Once the command has executed successfully, the web application will run on the default Beego port 8080.

Next, executing a GET request from the command line will give you a list of all the employees:

```
$ curl -X GET http://localhost:8080/employees
[
  {
    "id": 1,
    "firstName": "Foo",
    "lastName": "Bar"
  },
  {
    "id": 2,
    "firstName": "Baz",
    "lastName": "Qux"
  }
]
```

Let's understand the program we have written:

- import "github.com/astaxie/beego": Here, we imported Beego.
- type FirstController struct { beego.Controller }: Here, we defined the FirstController struct type, which contains an anonymous struct field of type beego.Controller because of which FirstController automatically acquires all the methods of beego.Controller.
- func (this *FirstController) GetEmployees() { this.Ctx.ResponseWriter.WriteHeader(200) this.Data["json"] = employees this.ServeJSON() }: Here, we defined the GetEmployees handler, which will execute for every GET request for the URL pattern /employees.

In Go, functions or handlers that start with a capital letter are exported functions, which means they are public and can be used outside the program. That's the reason we have defined all the functions in our program using a capital letter rather than in camel case.

Creating your first view

A view is a visual representation of a model. It accesses data through the model and specifies how that data should be presented. It maintains consistency in its presentation when the model changes, which can be either through a push model, where the view registers itself with the model for change notifications, or a pull model, where the view is responsible for calling the model when it needs to retrieve the most current data. In this recipe, we will learn how to create our first view to render the list of employees.

How to do it...

1. Move to `$GOPATH/src/my-first-beego-project/views` and create `dashboard.tpl` and copy the following content:

```html
<!DOCTYPE html>
<html>
  <body>
    <table border= "1" style="width:100%;">
      {{range .employees}}
      <tr>
        <td>{{.Id}}</td>
        <td>{{.FirstName}}</td>
        <td>{{.LastName}}</td>
      </tr>
      {{end}}
    </table>
  </body>
</html>
```

2. Move to `$GOPATH/src/my-first-beego-project/controllers` and edit `firstcontroller.go` to add the `Dashboard` handler, as follows:

```go
package controllers
import "github.com/astaxie/beego"
type FirstController struct
{
  beego.Controller
}
type Employee struct
{
  Id int `json:"id"`
  FirstName string `json:"firstName"`
  LastName string `json:"lastName"`
```

```
}
type Employees []Employee
var employees []Employee
func init()
{
  employees = Employees
  {
    Employee{Id: 1, FirstName: "Foo", LastName: "Bar"},
    Employee{Id: 2, FirstName: "Baz", LastName: "Qux"},
  }
}
...
func (this *FirstController) Dashbaord()
{
  this.Data["employees"] = employees
  this.TplName = "dashboard.tpl"
}
```

3. Move to `$GOPATH/src/my-first-beego-project/routers` and edit
   `router.go` to add the GET mapping `/dashboard`, which will be handled by
   the `Dashboard` handler defined in `FirstController`, as follows:

```
package routers
import
(
  "my-first-beego-project/controllers"
  "github.com/astaxie/beego"
)
func init()
{
  beego.Router("/", &controllers.MainController{})
  beego.Router("/employees", &controllers.FirstController{},
  "get:GetEmployees")
  beego.Router("/dashboard", &controllers.FirstController{},
  "get:Dashbaord")
}
```

4. Run the project using the following command:

```
$ bee run
```

How it works...

Once the command has executed successfully, the web application will run on the default Beego port 8080.

Browsing http://localhost:8080/dashboard will render the employee dashboard, as shown in the following screenshot:

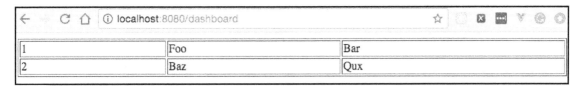

| 1 | Foo | Bar |
| 2 | Baz | Qux |

Creating your first session variable

Whenever we need to pass on the user data from one HTTP request to another, we can make use of HTTP sessions, which we will be covering in this recipe.

Getting ready...

This recipe assumes you have Redis installed and running locally on port 6379.

How to do it...

1. Install the github.com/astaxie/beego/session/redis package using the go get command, as follows:

    ```
    $ go get -u github.com/astaxie/beego/session/redis
    ```

2. Move to $GOPATH/src/my-first-beego-project/controllers and create sessioncontroller.go, where we will define handlers which make sure that only authenticated users can view the home page, as follows:

    ```
    package controllers
    import "github.com/astaxie/beego"
    type SessionController struct
    {
      beego.Controller
    ```

```
}
func (this *SessionController) Home()
{
  isAuthenticated := this.GetSession("authenticated")
  if isAuthenticated == nil || isAuthenticated == false
  {
    this.Ctx.WriteString("You are unauthorized to
    view the page.")
    return
  }
  this.Ctx.ResponseWriter.WriteHeader(200)
  this.Ctx.WriteString("Home Page")
}
func (this *SessionController) Login()
{
  this.SetSession("authenticated", true)
  this.Ctx.ResponseWriter.WriteHeader(200)
  this.Ctx.WriteString("You have successfully logged in.")
}
func (this *SessionController) Logout()
{
  this.SetSession("authenticated", false)
  this.Ctx.ResponseWriter.WriteHeader(200)
  this.Ctx.WriteString("You have successfully logged out.")
}
```

3. Move to `$GOPATH/src/my-first-beego-project/routers` and edit
`router.go` to add the GET mapping `/home`, `/login`, and `/logout`, which will be
handled by the `Home`, `Login`, and `Logout` handlers defined in
`FirstController`, respectively, as follows:

```
package routers
import
(
  "my-first-beego-project/controllers"
  "github.com/astaxie/beego"
)
func init()
{
  beego.Router("/", &controllers.MainController{})
  beego.Router("/employees", &controllers.FirstController{},
  "get:GetEmployees")
  beego.Router("/dashboard", &controllers.FirstController{},
  "get:Dashbaord")
  beego.Router("/home", &controllers.SessionController{},
  "get:Home")
  beego.Router("/login", &controllers.SessionController{},
```

```
    "get:Login")
    beego.Router("/logout", &controllers.SessionController{},
    "get:Logout")
}
```

4. Move to $GOPATH/src/my-first-beego-project and edit main.go to import github.com/astaxie/beego/session/redis, as follows:

```
package main
import
(
    _ "my-first-beego-project/routers"
    "github.com/astaxie/beego"
    _ "github.com/astaxie/beego/session/redis"
)
func main()
{
    beego.BConfig.WebConfig.DirectoryIndex = true
    beego.BConfig.WebConfig.StaticDir["/swagger"] = "swagger"
    beego.Run()
}
```

5. Switch on the session usage in $GOPATH/src/my-first-beego-project/conf/app.conf, as follows:

```
SessionOn = true
SessionProvider = "redis"
SessionProviderConfig = "127.0.0.1:6379"
```

6. Run the program using the following command:

```
$ bee run
```

How it works...

Once the command has executed successfully, the web application will run on the default Beego port 8080.

Next, we will execute a couple of commands to see how the session works. Firstly, we will access /home by executing the following command:

```
$ curl -X GET http://localhost:8080/home
```

This will give us an unauthorized access message as a response from the server:

```
You are unauthorized to view the page.
```

Apparently, we can't access it because we have to login into the application first, which will create a `beegosessionID`. Now let's log in to the application by executing the following command:

```
$ curl -X GET -i http://localhost:8080/login
```

This will result in the following response from the server:

```
    curl -X GET -i http://localhost:8080/login
HTTP/1.1 200 OK
Set-Cookie: beegosessionID=6e1c6f60141811f1371d7ea044f1c194; Path=/; HttpOnly
Date: Wed, 11 Apr 2018 08:51:38 GMT
Content-Length: 32
Content-Type: text/plain; charset=utf-8

You have successfully logged in.
```

Now we will use the cookie `beegosessionID` created as part of the `/login` request to access `/home`, as follows:

```
$ curl --cookie "beegosessionID=6e1c6f60141811f1371d7ea044f1c194"
http://localhost:8080/home

Home Page
```

Creating your first filter

Sometimes, we may want to perform logic either before an action method is called or after an action method runs. In that case, we use filters, which we will be covering in this recipe.

Filters are basically handlers which encapsulate the common functionality or the cross-cutting concern. We just define them once and then apply them to the different controllers and action methods.

How to do it...

1. Install the `github.com/astaxie/beego/context` package using the `go get` command, as follows:

```
$ go get github.com/astaxie/beego/context
```

2. Move to `$GOPATH/src/my-first-beego-project/filters` and create `firstfilter.go`, which runs before the `Controller`, and log the IP address and current timestamp, as follows:

```
package filters
import
(
  "fmt"
  "time"
  "github.com/astaxie/beego/context"
)
var LogManager = func(ctx *context.Context)
{
  fmt.Println("IP :: " + ctx.Request.RemoteAddr + ",
  Time :: " + time.Now().Format(time.RFC850))
}
```

3. Move to `$GOPATH/src/my-first-beego-project/routers` and edit `router.go` to add the GET mapping `/*`, which will be handled by the `LogManager` filter, as follows:

```
package routers
import
(
  "my-first-beego-project/controllers"
  "my-first-beego-project/filters"
  "github.com/astaxie/beego"
)
func init()
{
  beego.Router("/", &controllers.MainController{})
  ...
  beego.InsertFilter("/*", beego.BeforeRouter,
  filters.LogManager)
}
```

4. Run the program using the following command:

```
$ bee run
```

How it works...

Once the command has executed successfully, the web application will run on the default Beego port `8080`.

Next, we will execute a request to get all the employees by executing the following command:

```
$ curl -X GET http://localhost:8080/employees
[
  {
    "id": 1,
    "firstName": "Foo",
    "lastName": "Bar"
  },
  {
    "id": 2,
    "firstName": "Baz",
    "lastName": "Qux"
  }
]
```

Once the command has executed successfully, we can see the IP and timestamp printed in the application logs on the console, as follows:

```
      ___    \
| |_/ /        ___     ___
|  __ \ / _ \ / _ \
| |_/ /| __/| \__/
\____/ \___| \___|  v1.8.4
2018/04/03 16:16:08 INFO    ▶ 0001 Using 'my-first-beego-project' as 'appname'
2018/04/03 16:16:08 INFO    ▶ 0002 Initializing watcher...
2018/04/03 16:16:09 SUCCESS ▶ 0003 Built Successfully!
2018/04/03 16:16:09 INFO    ▶ 0004 Restarting 'my-first-beego-project'...
2018/04/03 16:16:09 SUCCESS ▶ 0005 './my-first-beego-project' is running...
2018/04/03 16:16:09.726 [I] [asm_amd64.s:2337] http server Running on http://:8080
2018/04/03 16:16:09.726 [I] [asm_amd64.s:2337] Admin server Running on localhost:8088
IP :: 127.0.0.1:63890, Time :: Tuesday, 03-Apr-18 16:16:25 IST
```

Using `beego.InsertFilter("/*", beego.BeforeRouter, filters.LogManager)`, we inserted a filter in an application which executes for the URL pattern `/*` before finding a router and that is handled by `LogManager`. Similar to `beego.BeforeRouter`, there are four other places where we can position the filters: `beego.BeforeStatic`, `beego.BeforeExec`, `beego.AfterExec`, and `beego.FinishRouter`.

Handling HTTP errors in Beego

Error handling is one of the most important aspects in a web application design because it helps in two ways. Firstly, it lets the application user know in a relatively friendly manner that something has gone wrong and they should contact the technical support department or someone from tech support should be notified. Secondly, it allows the programmer to put in some niceties to aid in the debugging of issues. In this recipe, we will learn how we can implement error handling in Beego.

How to do it...

1. Move to $GOPATH/src/my-first-beego-project/controllers and create errorcontroller.go, where we will define handlers to handle 404 and 500 HTTP errors as well as the handler to handle any generic error in an application, as follows:

```
package controllers
import "github.com/astaxie/beego"
type ErrorController struct
{
  beego.Controller
}
func (c *ErrorController) Error404()
{
  c.Data["content"] = "Page Not Found"
  c.TplName = "404.tpl"
}
func (c *ErrorController) Error500()
{
  c.Data["content"] = "Internal Server Error"
  c.TplName = "500.tpl"
}
func (c *ErrorController) ErrorGeneric()
{
  c.Data["content"] = "Some Error Occurred"
  c.TplName = "genericerror.tpl"
}
```

2. Move to `$GOPATH/src/my-first-beego-project/controllers` and edit `firstcontroller.go` to add the `GetEmployee` handler, which will get the ID from an HTTP request parameter, fetch the employee details from the static employee array, and return it as a response or throw the generic error if the requested ID does not exist, as follows:

```
package controllers
import "github.com/astaxie/beego"
type FirstController struct
{
  beego.Controller
}
type Employee struct
{
  Id int `json:"id"`
  FirstName string `json:"firstName"`
  LastName string `json:"lastName"`
}
type Employees []Employee
var employees []Employee
func init()
{
  employees = Employees
  {
    Employee{Id: 1, FirstName: "Foo", LastName: "Bar"},
    Employee{Id: 2, FirstName: "Baz", LastName: "Qux"},
  }
}
...
func (this *FirstController) GetEmployee()
{
  var id int
  this.Ctx.Input.Bind(&id, "id")
  var isEmployeeExist bool
  var emps []Employee
  for _, employee := range employees
  {
    if employee.Id == id
    {
      emps = append(emps, Employee{Id: employee.Id,
      FirstName: employee.FirstName, LastName:
      employee.LastName})
      isEmployeeExist = true
      break
    }
  }
  if !isEmployeeExist
```

```
  {
    this.Abort("Generic")
  }
  else
  {
    this.Data["employees"] = emps
    this.TplName = "dashboard.tpl"
  }
}
```

3. Move to `$GOPATH/src/my-first-beego-project/views` and create `genericerror.tpl` with the following content:

```
<!DOCTYPE html>
<html>
  <body>
    {{.content}}
  </body>
</html>
```

4. Run the program using the following command:

```
$ bee run
```

How it works...

Once the command has executed successfully, the web application will run on the default Beego port 8080.

Next, browsing `http://localhost:8080/employee?id=2` will give you the employee details, as shown in the following screenshot:

Whereas browsing `http://localhost:8080/employee?id=4` as follows:

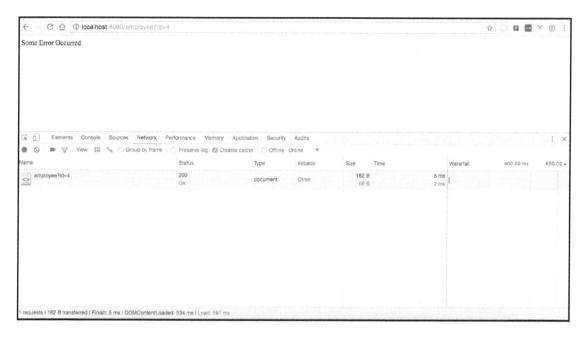

It will give you the error message as **Some Error Occurred**. This is because we have asked for details of the employee with the ID as 4, which does not exist in the static employee array, hence the generic error thrown from the server, which is handled by the `ErrorGeneric` handler defined in `errorcontroller.go`.

Implementing caching in Beego

Caching data in a web application is sometimes necessary to avoid requesting the static data from a database or external service again and again. In this recipe, we will learn how we can implement caching in a Beego application.

Beego supports four cache providers: `file`, `Memcache`, `memory`, and `Redis`. In this recipe, we will be working with the framework default cache provider, which is a `memory` cache provider.

How to do it...

1. Install the `github.com/astaxie/beego/cache` package using the `go get` command, as follows:

```
$ go get github.com/astaxie/beego/cache
```

2. Move to `$GOPATH/src/my-first-beego-project/controllers` and create `cachecontroller.go`, where we will define the `GetFromCache` handler, which will get the value for a key from a cache and write it to an HTTP response, as follows:

```
package controllers
import
(
  "fmt"
  "time"
  "github.com/astaxie/beego"
  "github.com/astaxie/beego/cache"
)
type CacheController struct
{
  beego.Controller
}
var beegoCache cache.Cache
var err error
func init()
{
  beegoCache, err = cache.NewCache("memory",
  `{"interval":60}`)
  beegoCache.Put("foo", "bar", 100000*time.Second)
}
func (this *CacheController) GetFromCache()
{
  foo := beegoCache.Get("foo")
  this.Ctx.WriteString("Hello " + fmt.Sprintf("%v", foo))
}
```

3. Move to $GOPATH/src/my-first-beego-project/routers and edit router.go to add the GET mapping /getFromCache, which will be handled by the GetFromCache handler defined in a CacheController, as follows:

```
package routers
import
(
  "my-first-beego-project/controllers"
  "my-first-beego-project/filters"
  "github.com/astaxie/beego"
)
func init()
{
  beego.Router("/", &controllers.MainController{})
  ...
  beego.Router("/getFromCache", &controllers.
  CacheController{}, "get:GetFromCache")
}
```

4. Run the program using the following command:

```
$ bee run
```

How it works...

Once the command has executed successfully, the web application will run on the default Beego port 8080.

On application startup, the key with the name `foo` with the value as `bar` will be added to the cache. Next, browsing `http://localhost:8080/getFromCache` will read a `foo` key value from the cache, append it to **Hello**, and display it on the browser, as shown in the following screenshot:

Monitoring the Beego application

Once the Beego application is up and running, we can easily monitor application request statistics, performance, health checks, tasks, and the configuration status through its admin dashboard. We will learn how to do this in this recipe.

How to do it...

1. Enable the application live monitor by adding `EnableAdmin = true` in `$GOPATH/src/my-first-beego-project/conf/app.conf`, as follows:

```
appname = my-first-beego-project
...
EnableAdmin = true
..
```

Optionally, change the port it listens on, by adding fields in `$GOPATH/src/my-first-beego-project/conf/app.conf`:

```
AdminAddr = "localhost"
AdminPort = 8088
```

2. Run the program using the following command:

```
$ bee run
```

How it works...

Once the command has executed successfully, the web application will run on the default Beego port `8080` and browsing `http://localhost:8088/` will render the admin dashboard, as shown in the following screenshot:

Browsing `http://localhost:8088/qps` will show us the request statistics of an application, as shown in the following screenshot:

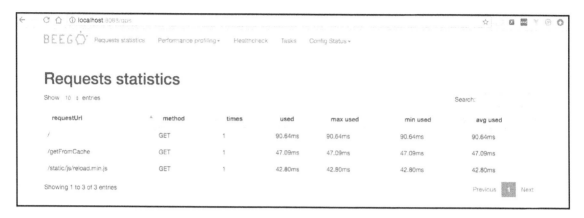

Deploying the Beego application on a local machine

Once the application development is over, we have to deploy it to make it available for use by the end users, which can be done either locally or remotely. In this recipe, we will learn how we can deploy our Beego application on a local machine.

How to do it...

1. Because the application created by `bee` is in the development mode by default and it's always a best practice to run an application in the production mode on the public facing servers, we have to change the `RunMode` as `prod` in `$GOPATH/src/my-first-beego-project/conf/app.conf`, as follows:

   ```
   beego.RunMode = "prod"
   ```

2. Include static files, configuration files, and templates as part of the Beego application bytecode file in a separate directory by executing the following commands:

```
$ mkdir $GOPATH/my-first-beego-app-deployment
$ cp my-first-beego-project $GOPATH/my-first-beego-app-deployment
$ cp -fr views $GOPATH/my-first-beego-app-deployment
$ cp -fr static $GOPATH/my-first-beego-app-deployment
$ cp -fr conf $GOPATH/my-first-beego-app-deployment
```

3. Move to $GOPATH/my-first-beego-app-deployment and use the nohup command to run an application as a backend process, as follows:

```
$ cd $GOPATH/my-first-beego-app-deployment
$ nohup ./my-first-beego-project &
```

How it works...

Once the command has executed successfully, the web application will run on the default Beego port 8080, and browsing http://localhost:8080/ will render the welcome page of the application, as shown in the following screenshot:

Deploying the Beego application with Nginx

In the previous recipe, we learned how we can run the Beego application locally. In this recipe, we will be deploying the same application with `Nginx`.

Getting ready...

This recipe assumes you have `Nginx` installed and running on port `80`. For me, it's installed at `/Users/ArpitAggarwal/nginx`.

How to do it...

1. Open the Nginx configuration file at `/Users/ArpitAggarwal/nginx/conf/nginx.conf` and replace the `location` block under `server` with the following content:

```
location /
{
  # root html;
  # index index.html index.htm;
  proxy_pass http://localhost:8080/;
}
```

2. Start Nginx by executing the following command:

```
$ cd /Users/ArpitAggarwal/nginx/sbin
$ ./nginx
```

3. Run the Beego application by executing the following command:

```
$ bee run
```

How it works...

Once the command has executed successfully, browsing `http://localhost:80/` will render the welcome page of the application, as shown in the following screenshot:

Working with Go and Docker

9

In this chapter, we will cover the following recipes:

- Building your first Go Docker image
- Running your first Go Docker container
- Pushing your Docker image to the Docker Registry
- Creating your first user-defined bridge network
- Running a MySQL Docker image on a user-defined bridge network
- Building a Go web application Docker image
- Running a web application Docker container linked with a MySQL Docker container on a user-defined bridge network

Introduction

With organizations moving towards DevOps, Docker has started to gain popularity as well. Docker allows for packaging an application with all of its dependencies into a standardized unit for software development. And if that unit runs on your local machine, we can guarantee that it will run exactly the same way, anywhere from QA, to staging, and to production environments. With the knowledge of the concepts covered in this chapter, we will be able to write Docker images and deploy Docker containers with ease.

In this chapter, we will learn how to create a Docker image and Docker containers to deploy a simple Go web application, following which we will be looking at how we can save the container to an image and push it to the Docker registry, along with some basic concepts of Docker networking.

As we are going to work with Docker, I assume it's installed and running on your local machine.

Building your first Go Docker image

A Docker image is the filesystem and configuration of our application and is further used to create Docker containers. There are two ways by which a Docker image can be created, which is either from scratch or from a parent image. In this recipe, we will learn how to create a Docker image from a parent image. This means an image created basically refers to the contents of its parent and subsequent declarations in the `Dockerfile` modify the parent image.

Getting ready...

Verify whether `Docker` and `Docker Machine` are installed by executing the following commands:

```
$ docker --version
Docker version 18.03.0-ce, build 0520e24

$ docker-machine --version
docker-machine version 0.14.0, build 89b8332
```

How to do it...

1. Create `http-server.go`, where we will create a simple HTTP server that will render **Hello World!** browsing `http://docker-machine-ip:8080` or executing `curl -X GET http://docker-machine-ip:8080` from the command line, as follows:

```go
package main
import
(
  "fmt"
  "log"
  "net/http"
)
const
(
  CONN_HOST = "localhost"
  CONN_PORT = "8080"
)
func helloWorld(w http.ResponseWriter, r *http.Request)
```

```
{
  fmt.Fprintf(w, "Hello World!")
}
func main()
{
  http.HandleFunc("/", helloWorld)
  err := http.ListenAndServe(CONN_HOST+":"+CONN_PORT, nil)
  if err != nil
  {
    log.Fatal("error starting http server : ", err)
    return
  }
}
```

2. Create a `DockerFile`, which is a text file that contains all the commands needed to build an image. We will use `golang:1.9.2` as the base, or the parent image, which we have specified using the `FROM` directive in the `Dockerfile`, as follows:

```
FROM golang:1.9.2
ENV SRC_DIR=/go/src/github.com/arpitaggarwal/
ENV GOBIN=/go/bin

WORKDIR $GOBIN

# Add the source code:
ADD . $SRC_DIR

RUN cd /go/src/;

RUN go install github.com/arpitaggarwal/;
ENTRYPOINT ["./arpitaggarwal"]

EXPOSE 8080
```

With everything in place, the directory structure should look like the following:

3. Build a Docker image from the `Dockerfile` executing the `docker build` command with the image name as `golang-image` using the `-t` flag, as follows:

```
$ docker build --no-cache=true -t golang-image .
```

Once the preceding command has executed successfully, it will render the following output:

```
Sending build context to Docker daemon 3.072 kB
Step 1/9 : FROM golang:1.9.2
 ---> 1a34fad76b34
Step 2/9 : ENV SRC_DIR=/go/src/github.com/arpitaggarwal/
 ---> Running in 5c9f11938ed6
 ---> f836db6f231f
Step 3/9 : ENV GOBIN=/go/bin
 ---> Running in 496961141a2c
 ---> faa3a29eb48f
Step 4/9 : WORKDIR $GOBIN
 ---> 816c09ec84ce
Step 5/9 : ADD . $SRC_DIR
 ---> 9634ae0cf48e
Step 6/9 : RUN cd /go/src/;
 ---> Running in 51b204150e3c
 ---> 8c5653df7b73
Step 7/9 : RUN go install github.com/arpitaggarwal/;
 ---> Running in 82b94378ae7c
 ---> 5342329603b2
Step 8/9 : ENTRYPOINT ["./arpitaggarwal"]
 ---> Running in fadbf159c613
 ---> 3b56a627e2f8
Step 9/9 : EXPOSE 8080
 ---> Running in 95abb9d08245
 ---> bd2a74aec5e9
Removing intermediate container 82b94378ae7c
Removing intermediate container fadbf159c613
Removing intermediate container 95abb9d08245
Removing intermediate container 5c9f11938ed6
Removing intermediate container 496961141a2c
Removing intermediate container 260a8fe27095
Removing intermediate container 51b204150e3c
Successfully built bd2a74aec5e9
Successfully tagged golang-image:latest
```

If you are building an image behind a corporate proxy, you will probably have to provide the proxy settings. You can do this by adding environment variables using the ENV statement in the `Dockerfile`, which we often call as a runtime customization, as follows:

```
FROM golang:1.9.2
....
ENV http_proxy "http://proxy.corp.com:80"
ENV https_proxy "http://proxy.corp.com:80"
...
```

We can also pass the proxy settings at build time to the builder using the `--build-arg <varname>=<value>` flag, which is called as a build time customization, as follows:

```
$ docker build --no-cache=true --build-arg
http_proxy="http://proxy.corp.com:80" -t golang-image .
```

How it works...

Verify whether the Docker image has been created successfully by executing the following command:

```
$ docker images
```

This will list all the top-level images, their repositories, tags, and their size, as shown in the following screenshot:

```
REPOSITORY         TAG           IMAGE ID        CREATED         SIZE
golang-image       latest        bd2a74aec5e9    8 minutes ago   739.4 MB
golang             1.9.2         1a34fad76b34    5 months ago    733.3 MB
golang             <none>        1a34fad76b34    5 months ago    733.3 MB
```

Let's understand the `Dockerfile` we have created:

- `FROM golang:1.9.2`: The `FROM` instruction specifies the base image, which is, for us `golang:1.9.2`
- `ENV SRC_DIR=/go/src/github.com/arpitaggarwal/`: Here, we are setting the Go source code directory as an environment variable using the `ENV` statement
- `ENV GOBIN=/go/bin`: Here, we are setting the `GOBIN` or a directory to generate executable binaries as an environment variable using the `ENV` statement
- `WORKDIR $GOBIN`: The `WORKDIR` instruction sets the working directory for any `RUN`, `CMD`, `ENTRYPOINT`, `COPY` and `ADD` statements, which is `/go/bin` for our image
- `ADD . $SRC_DIR`: Here, we copy `http-server.go` from the current directory on our host machine to the `/go/src/github.com/arpitaggarwal/` directory of `golang-image` using the `ADD` statement

- RUN cd /go/src/: Here, we change the current directory to /go/src/ in a golang-image using the RUN statement
- RUN go install github.com/arpitaggarwal/: Here, we compile /go/src/github.com/arpitaggarwal/http-server.go and generate an executable binary file of it in the /go/bin directory
- ENTRYPOINT ["./arpitaggarwal"]: Here, we are specifying the executable binary generated to run as an executable when running a container
- EXPOSE 8080: The EXPOSE instruction informs Docker that the container that we will create from an image will listen on the network port 8080 at runtime

Running your first Go Docker container

A Docker container includes an application and all of its dependencies. It shares the kernel with other containers and runs as an isolated process in the user space on the host operating system. To run the actual application, we have to create and run the containers from an image, which we will be covering in this recipe.

How to do it...

Execute the docker run command to create and run a Docker container from the golang-image, assigning the container name as golang-container using the –name flag, as follows:

```
$ docker run -d -p 8080:8080 --name golang-container -it golang-image
  9eb53d8d41a237ac216c9bb0f76b4b47d2747fab690569ef6ff4b216e6aab486
```

The –d flag specified in the docker run command starts the container in a daemon mode and the hash string at the end represents the ID of the golang-container.

How it works...

Verify whether the Docker container has been created and is running successfully by executing the following command:

```
$ docker ps
```

Once the preceding command has executed successfully, it will give us the running Docker container details, as shown in the following screenshot:

CONTAINER ID	IMAGE	COMMAND	CREATED	STATUS	PORTS	NAMES
f632ef0ee754	golang-image	"./arpitaggarwal"	7 seconds ago	Up 6 seconds	0.0.0.0:8080->8080/tcp	golang-container

> To list all the Docker containers, whether they are running or not, we have to pass an additional flag, `-a`, as `docker ps -a`.

Browse `http://localhost:8080/` or execute a `GET` call from the command line, as follows:

```
$ curl -X GET http://localhost:8080/
  Hello World!
```

This will give us **Hello World!** as a response, which means the HTTP server is listening inside a Docker container at port `8080`.

Pushing your Docker image to the Docker Registry

Once a Docker image has been created, it's always best practice to store or save the image so that the next time you have to boot up the containers from your custom image, you don't have to bother about or remember the steps you performed earlier while creating it.

You can save an image either on a local machine or in an artifactory or to any of the public or private Docker Registries, such as Docker Hub, Quay, Google Container Registry, AWS Container Registry, and so on. In this recipe, we will learn how to save or push an image which we have created in one of our previous recipes to the Docker Hub.

> See the *Building your first Go Docker image* recipe.

How to do it...

1. Create your account on the Docker Hub (`https://hub.docker.com/`).

2. Login into the Docker Hub from the command line by executing the `docker login` command, as follows:

```
$ docker login --username arpitaggarwal --password XXXXX
Login Succeeded
```

3. Tag the `golang-image`:

```
$ docker tag golang-image arpitaggarwal/golang-image
```

4. Verify whether the image has been tagged successfully by executing the `docker images` command:

```
$ docker images
```

Executing the preceding command will list all the Docker images, as shown in the following screenshot:

```
→  build-go-docker-image git:(master) x docker images
REPOSITORY                    TAG          IMAGE ID            CREATED              SIZE
arpitaggarwal/golang-image    latest       8e38322fb8e3        About an hour ago    739MB
golang-image                  latest       8e38322fb8e3        About an hour ago    739MB
golang                        1.9.2        138bd936fa29        3 months ago         733MB
```

5. Push the tagged image to the Docker Hub by executing the `docker push` command, as follows:

```
$ docker push arpitaggarwal/golang-image
The push refers to a repository [docker.io/arpitaggarwal
/golang-image]
4db0afeaa6dd: Pushed
4e648ebe6cf2: Pushed
6bfc813a3812: Mounted from library/golang
e1e44e9665b9: Mounted from library/golang
1654abf914f4: Mounted from library/golang
2a55a2194a6c: Mounted from library/golang
52c175f1a4b1: Mounted from library/golang
faccc7315fd9: Pushed
e38b8aef9521: Mounted from library/golang
```

```
a75caa09eb1f: Mounted from library/golang
latest: digest:
sha256:ca8f0a1530d3add72ad4e328e51235ef70c5fb8f38bde906a378d74d2b75
c8a8 size: 2422
```

How it works...

To verify whether an image has been pushed successfully to the Docker Hub, browse `https://hub.docker.com/`, sign in using your credentials, and, once logged in, you will see the tagged image, as shown in the following screenshot:

If you performed any changes to the Docker container and want to persist them as well as part of an image, then first you have to commit the changes to a new image or to the same image using the `docker commit` command before tagging and pushing it to the Docker Hub, as follows:

```
$ docker commit <container-id> golang-image-new
$ docker tag golang-image-new arpitaggarwal/golang-image
$ docker push arpitaggarwal/golang-image
```

Creating your first user-defined bridge network

Whenever we want to connect one Docker container to another Docker container by the container name, then first we have to create a user-defined network. This is because Docker does not support automatic service discovery on the default bridge network. In this recipe, we will learn how to create our own bridge network.

How to do it...

Execute the `docker network` command to create a bridge network with the name as `my-bridge-network`, as follows:

```
$ docker network create my-bridge-network
325bca66cc2ccb98fb6044b1da90ed4b6b0f29b54c4588840e259fb7b6505331
```

How it works...

Verify whether `my-bridge-network` has been created successfully by executing the following command:

```
$ docker network ls
NETWORK ID NAME DRIVER
20dc090404cb bridge bridge
9fa39d9bb674 host host
325bca66cc2c my-bridge-network bridge
f36203e11372 none null
```

To see detailed information about `my-bridge-network`, run the `docker network inspect` command followed by the network name, as follows:

```
$ docker network inspect my-bridge-network
[
    {
        "Name": "my-bridge-network",
        "Id": "325bca66cc2ccb98fb6044b1da90ed4b6b0
f29b54c4588840e259fb7b6505331",
        "Scope": "local",
        "Driver": "bridge",
        "EnableIPv6": false,
        "IPAM":
```

```
{
  "Driver": "default",
  "Options": {},
  "Config":
  [
    {
      "Subnet": "172.18.0.0/16",
      "Gateway": "172.18.0.1"
    }
  ]
},
"Internal": false,
"Containers": {},
"Options": {},
"Labels": {}
}
]
```

Running a MySQL Docker image on a user-defined bridge network

Whenever we run a Docker image to create and boot up a container, it uses the default bridge network, which Docker creates during installation. To run an image on a specific network, which may be either user-defined or one of the other two networks that Docker creates automatically, host or none, we have to provide the additional --net flag with the value as the network name as part of the docker run command.

In this recipe, we will run a MySQL image on the user-defined bridge network that we created in the previous recipe, passing the --net flag value as my-bridge-network.

How to do it...

Execute the docker run command to create and run a MySQL Docker container from the mysql:latest image, assigning the container name as mysql-container using the --name flag, as follows:

```
$ docker run --net=my-bridge-network -p 3306:3306 --name mysql-container -e
MYSQL_ROOT_PASSWORD=my-pass -d mysql:latest
  c3ca3e6f253efa40b1e691023155ab3f37eb07b767b1744266ac4ae85fca1722
```

The --net flag specified in the docker run command connects mysql-container to my-bridge-network. The -p flag specified in the docker run command publishes the container's 3306 port to the host 3306 port. The -e flag specified in the docker run command sets the MYSQL_ROOT_PASSWORD value as my-pass, which is an environment variable of the mysql:latest image. The -d flag specified in the docker run command starts the container in a daemon mode, and the hash string at the end represents the ID of the mysql-container.

How it works...

Verify whether the Docker container has been created and is running successfully by executing the following command:

```
$ docker ps
 CONTAINER ID IMAGE COMMAND CREATED STATUS PORTS NAMES
 f2ec80f82056 mysql:latest "docker-entrypoint.sh" 8 seconds ago Up 6
seconds 0.0.0.0:3306->3306/tcp mysql-container
```

Inspecting the my-bridge-network again will show us the mysql-container details in the Containers section, as follows:

```
$ docker network inspect my-bridge-network
[
  {
    "Name": "my-bridge-network",
    "Id": "325bca66cc2ccb98fb6044b1da90ed
    4b6b0f29b54c4588840e259fb7b6505331",
    "Scope": "local",
    "Driver": "bridge",
    "EnableIPv6": false,
    "IPAM":
    {
      "Driver": "default",
      "Options": {},
      "Config":
      [
        {
          "Subnet": "172.18.0.0/16",
          "Gateway": "172.18.0.1"
        }
      ]
    },
    "Internal": false,
    "Containers":
```

```
{
  "f2ec80f820566707ba7b18ce12ca7a65
  c87fa120fd4221e11967131656f68e59":
  {
    "Name": "mysql-container",
    "EndpointID": "58092b80bd34135d94154e4d8a8f5806bad
    601257cfbe28e53b5d7161da3b350",
    "MacAddress": "02:42:ac:12:00:02",
    "IPv4Address": "172.18.0.2/16",
    "IPv6Address": ""
  }
},
"Options": {},
"Labels": {}
}
]
```

Building a Go web application Docker image

In this recipe, we will build a Docker image that connects to the MySQL database instance running in a separate Docker container.

How to do it...

1. Create `http-server.go`, where we will create a simple HTTP server and a handler which will give us the current database details, such as machine IP, hostname, port, and selected database, as follows:

```
package main
import
(
  "bytes"
  "database/sql"
  "fmt"
  "log"
  "net/http"
  "github.com/go-sql-driver/mysql"
  "github.com/gorilla/mux"
)
var db *sql.DB
var connectionError error
const
```

```
(
  CONN_PORT = "8080"
  DRIVER_NAME = "mysql"
  DATA_SOURCE_NAME = "root:my-pass@tcp(mysql-container:3306)/mysql"
)
func init()
{
  db, connectionError = sql.Open(DRIVER_NAME, DATA_SOURCE_NAME)
  if connectionError != nil
  {
    log.Fatal("error connecting to database : ", connectionError)
  }
}
func getDBInfo(w http.ResponseWriter, r *http.Request)
{
  rows, err := db.Query("SELECT SUBSTRING_INDEX(USER(),
  '@', -1) AS ip, @@hostname as hostname, @@port as port,
  DATABASE() as current_database;")
  if err != nil
  {
    log.Print("error executing database query : ", err)
    return
  }
  var buffer bytes.Buffer
  for rows.Next()
  {
    var ip string
    var hostname string
    var port string
    var current_database string
    err = rows.Scan(&ip, &hostname, &port, &current_database)
    buffer.WriteString("IP :: " + ip + " | HostName :: " +
    hostname + " | Port :: " + port + " | Current
    Database :: " + current_database)
  }
  fmt.Fprintf(w, buffer.String())
}
func main()
{
  router := mux.NewRouter()
  router.HandleFunc("/", getDBInfo).Methods("GET")
  defer db.Close()
  err := http.ListenAndServe(":"+CONN_PORT, router)
  if err != nil
  {
    log.Fatal("error starting http server : ", err)
    return
  }
```

```
}
```

2. Create a `DockerFile`, which is a text file that contains all the commands needed to build an image, as follows:

```
FROM golang:1.9.2

ENV SRC_DIR=/go/src/github.com/arpitaggarwal/
ENV GOBIN=/go/bin

WORKDIR $GOBIN

ADD . $SRC_DIR

RUN cd /go/src/;
RUN go get github.com/go-sql-driver/mysql;
RUN go get github.com/gorilla/mux;

RUN go install github.com/arpitaggarwal/;
ENTRYPOINT ["./arpitaggarwal"]

EXPOSE 8080
```

With everything in place, the directory structure should look like the following:

3. Build a Docker image from the `Dockerfile` executing the `docker build` command with the image name as `web-application-image` using the `-t` flag, as follows:

```
$ docker build --no-cache=true -t web-application-image .
```

Once the preceding command has executed successfully, it will render the following output:

```
Sending build context to Docker daemon 4.096 kB
Step 1/11 : FROM golang:1.9.2
 ---> 1a34fad76b34
Step 2/11 : ENV SRC_DIR=/go/src/github.com/arpitaggarwal/
 ---> Running in 6187b07590f1
 ---> 209f2d60e094
Step 3/11 : ENV GOBIN=/go/bin
 ---> Running in c9ef7e31b8a8
 ---> 15c8db245ffa
Step 4/11 : WORKDIR $GOBIN
 ---> 7e2f82fa1ff8
Step 5/11 : ADD . $SRC_DIR
 ---> 5d186d741391
Step 6/11 : RUN cd /go/src/;
 ---> Running in 598aa85da523
 ---> b54a398b5423
Step 7/11 : RUN go get github.com/go-sql-driver/mysql;
 ---> Running in d8164949ff3a
 ---> 133f3ced8881
Step 8/11 : RUN go get github.com/gorilla/mux;
 ---> Running in caa0e603a0ec
 ---> a3a1dcf87e8c
Step 9/11 : RUN go install github.com/arpitaggarwal/;
 ---> Running in 6d29d56eeebc
 ---> c455f356e132
Step 10/11 : ENTRYPOINT ["./arpitaggarwal"]
 ---> Running in 279c1f75e9ef
 ---> af9e0a261fe7
Step 11/11 : EXPOSE 8080
 ---> Running in ea61d0b01cba
 ---> 7f36e951babd
Removing intermediate container c9ef7e31b8a8
Removing intermediate container 1ee190aea442
Removing intermediate container 279c1f75e9ef
Removing intermediate container ea61d0b01cba
Removing intermediate container 6187b07590f1
Removing intermediate container 598aa85da523
Removing intermediate container d8164949ff3a
Removing intermediate container caa0e603a0ec
Removing intermediate container 6d29d56eeebc
Successfully built 7f36e951babd
Successfully tagged web-application-image:latest
```

How it works...

Verify whether the Docker image has been created successfully by executing the following command:

```
$ docker images
```

This will list all the top-level images, their repositories, tags, and their size, as shown in the following screenshot:

```
REPOSITORY              TAG         IMAGE ID        CREATED         SIZE
web-application-image   latest      7f36e951babd    2 minutes ago   742.8 MB
golang-image            latest      bd2a74aec5e9    16 minutes ago  739.4 MB
golang                  1.9.2       1a34fad76b34    5 months ago    733.3 MB
golang                  <none>      1a34fad76b34    5 months ago    733.3 MB
```

The `Dockerfile` we created in this recipe is exactly the same as the one we created in one of our previous recipes, except for the two additional commands that install the Go MySQL Driver and the Gorilla Mux URL router while building the image, as follows:

```
. . .
RUN go get github.com/go-sql-driver/mysql;
RUN go get github.com/gorilla/mux;
. . .
```

 See the *Building your first Go Docker image* recipe.

Running a web application Docker container linked with a MySQL Docker container on a user-defined bridge network

In this recipe, we will learn how to run a Go web application Docker image to create a container which will communicate with the MYSQL database instance running in a separate Docker container.

As we know Docker does not support automatic service discovery on the default bridge network, we will be using the user-defined network that we created in one of our previous recipes to run a Go web application Docker image.

How to do it...

Execute the docker run command to create a web application Docker container from the web-application-image, assigning the container name as web-application-container using the --name flag, as follows:

```
$ docker run --net=my-bridge-network -p 8090:8080 --name web-application-
container -d web-application-image
  ef9c73396e9f9e04c94b7327e8f02cf57ce5f0cd674791e2805c86c70e5b9564
```

The --net flag specified in the docker run command connects the mysql-container to the my-bridge-network. The -p flag specified in the docker run command publishes the container's 8080 port to the host 8080 port. The -d flag specified in the docker run command starts the container in a daemon mode and the hash string at the end represents the ID of the web-application-container.

How it works...

Verify whether the Docker container has been created and is running successfully by executing the following command:

```
$ docker ps
```

This will render the following output:

```
build-go-webapp-docker-image git:(master) docker ps
CONTAINER ID   IMAGE                  COMMAND              CREATED          STATUS            PORTS                    NAMES
0b8be2be1987   web-application-image  "./arpitaggarwal"    8 seconds ago    Up 21 seconds     0.0.0.0:8090->8080/tcp   web-application-container
a3c54f28ff47   mysql:latest           "docker-entrypoint.s…"  19 minutes ago   Up 19 minutes     0.0.0.0:3306->3306/tcp   mysql-container
d418ab1623c0   golang-image           "./arpitaggarwal"    About an hour ago  Up About an hour  0.0.0.0:8080->8080/tcp   golang-container
```

Browsing http://localhost:8090/ as will give us the machine IP, hostname, port, and current database details as the response:

```
← C ⌂ ⓘ localhost:8090

IP :: 172.18.0.3 | HostName :: a3c54f28ff47 | Port :: 3306 | Current Database :: mysql
```

Moreover, inspecting my-bridge-network again will show us the mysql-container and web-application-container details in the Containers section, as follows:

```
$ docker network inspect my-bridge-network
[
  {
```

```
    "Name": "my-bridge-network",
    "Id": "325bca66cc2ccb98fb6044b1da90ed4b6b0
    f29b54c4588840e259fb7b6505331",
    "Scope": "local",
    "Driver": "bridge",
    "EnableIPv6": false,
    "IPAM":
    {
       "Driver": "default",
       "Options": {},
       "Config":
       [
          {
             "Subnet": "172.18.0.0/16",
             "Gateway": "172.18.0.1"
          }
       ]
    },
    "Internal": false,
    "Containers":
    {
       "08ce8f20c3205fa3e421083fa1077b
       673cdd10fd5be34f5ef431fead06219019":
       {
          "Name": "web-application-container",
          "EndpointID": "d22f7076cf037ef0f0057ffb9fec
          0a07e07b44b442182544731db1ad10db87e4",
          "MacAddress": "02:42:ac:12:00:03",
          "IPv4Address": "172.18.0.3/16",
          "IPv6Address": ""
       },
       "f2ec80f820566707ba7b18ce12ca7a65
       c87fa120fd4221e11967131656f68e59":
       {
          "Name": "mysql-container",
          "EndpointID": "58092b80bd34135d94154e4d8
          a8f5806bad601257cfbe28e53b5d7161da3b350",
          "MacAddress": "02:42:ac:12:00:02",
          "IPv4Address": "172.18.0.2/16",
          "IPv6Address": ""
       }
    },
    "Options": {},
    "Labels": {}
  }
]
```

Securing a Go Web Application **10**

In this chapter, we will cover the following recipes:

- Creating a private key and SSL certificate using OpenSSL
- Moving an HTTP server to HTTPS
- Defining REST APIs and routes
- Creating a JSON web token
- Securing a RESTful service using a JSON web token
- Preventing cross-site request forgery in Go web applications

Introduction

Securing web applications is one of the most important aspects, besides creating applications, that we will be learning about in this chapter. Application security is a very wide topic and can be implemented in various ways that are beyond the scope of this chapter.

In this chapter, we will just focus on how we can move our Go web application from the HTTP protocol to HTTPS, which is often called **HTTP + TLS (Transport Layer Security)**, along with securing Go web application REST endpoints using **JSON web tokens (JWTs)**, and protecting our application from **cross-site request forgery (CSRF)** attacks.

Creating a private key and SSL certificate using OpenSSL

To move a server running on HTTP to HTTPS, the first thing we have to do is to get the SSL certificate, which may be either self-signed or a certificate signed by a trusted certificate authority such as Comodo, Symantec, or GoDaddy.

To get the SSL certificate signed by a trusted certificate authority, we have to provide them with a **Certificate Signing Request** (**CSR**), which mainly consists of the public key of a key pair and some additional information, whereas a self-signed certificate is a certificate that you can issue to yourself, signed with its own private key.

Self-signed certificates can be used to encrypt data as well as CA-signed certificates, but the users will be displayed with a warning that says that the certificate is not trusted by their computer or browser. Therefore, you should not use them for the production or public servers.

In this recipe, we will learn how to create a private key, a certificate-signing request, and a self-signed certificate.

Getting ready...

This recipe assumes you have `openssl` installed on your machine. To verify that it is installed, execute the following command:

```
$ openssl
OpenSSL> exit
```

How to do it...

1. Generate a private key and certificate signing request using `openssl` by executing the following command:

```
$ openssl req -newkey rsa:2048 -nodes -keyout domain.key -out
domain.csr -subj "/C=IN/ST=Mumbai/L=Andheri
East/O=Packt/CN=packtpub.com"
```

This will give the following output:

```
Generating a 2048 bit RSA private key
...........+++
.................................+++
writing new private key to 'domain.key'
-----
```

2. Generate a certificate and sign it with the private key we just created by executing the following command:

```
$ openssl req -key domain.key -new -x509 -days 365 -out domain.crt
-subj "/C=IN/ST=Mumbai/L=Andheri East/O=Packt/CN=packtpub.com"
```

How it works...

Once the command has executed successfully, we can see domain.key, domain.csr, and domain.crt generated, where domain.key is a 2,048-bit RSA private key that is used to sign the SSL certificate, and domain.crt and domain.csr are certificate-signing requests that consist of the public key of a key pair with some additional information, which is inserted into the certificate when it is signed.

Let's understand the command we executed to generate a certificate-signing request:

- The -newkey rsa:2048 option creates a new certificate request and a new private key that should be 2,048-bit, generated using the RSA algorithm.
- The -nodes option specifies that the private key created will not be encrypted with a passphrase.
- The -keyout domain.key option specifies the filename to write the newly created private key to.
- The -out domain.csr option specifies the output filename to write to, or the standard output by default.
- The -subj option replaces a subject field of the input request with specified data and outputs a modified request. If we do not specify this option, then we have to answer the CSR information prompt by OpenSSL to complete the process.

Next, we will understand the command we executed to generate the certificate and sign it with the private key, as follows:

```
openssl req -key domain.key -new -x509 -days 365 -out domain.crt -subj
"/C=IN/ST=Mumbai/L=Andheri East/O=Packt/CN=packtpub.com"
```

The -key option specifies the file to read the private key from. The -x509 option outputs a self-signed certificate instead of a certificate request. The -days 365 option specifies the number of days to certify the certificate for. The default is 30 days.

Moving an HTTP server to HTTPS

Once the web application development is over, it's likely that we will deploy it to the servers. While deploying, it is always recommended to run the web application on an HTTPS protocol rather than HTTP, especially for the servers that are publicly exposed. In this recipe, we will learn how we can do this in Go.

How to do it...

1. Create `https-server.go`, where we will define a handler that will just write **Hello World!** to an HTTP response stream for all HTTPS requests, as follows:

```
package main
import
(
  "fmt"
  "log"
  "net/http"
)
const
(
  CONN_HOST = "localhost"
  CONN_PORT = "8443"
  HTTPS_CERTIFICATE = "domain.crt"
  DOMAIN_PRIVATE_KEY = "domain.key"
)
func helloWorld(w http.ResponseWriter, r *http.Request)
{
  fmt.Fprintf(w, "Hello World!")
}
func main()
{
  http.HandleFunc("/", helloWorld)
  err := http.ListenAndServeTLS(CONN_HOST+":"+CONN_PORT,
  HTTPS_CERTIFICATE, DOMAIN_PRIVATE_KEY, nil)
  if err != nil
  {
    log.Fatal("error starting https server : ", err)
    return
  }
}
```

2. Run the program with the following command:

```
$ go run https-server.go
```

How it works...

Once we run the program, the HTTPS server will start locally listening on port 8443.

Browsing https://localhost:8443/ will give us **Hello World!** as a response from the server:

Moreover, executing a GET request from the command line passing the --insecure flag with curl will skip the certificate validation, as we are using a self-signed certificate:

```
$ curl -X GET https://localhost:8443/ --insecure
Hello World!
```

Let's understand the program we have written:

- const (CONN_HOST = "localhost" CONN_PORT = "8443" HTTPS_CERTIFICATE = "domain.crt" DOMAIN_PRIVATE_KEY = "domain.key"): Here, we declared four constants - CONN_HOST with the value as localhost, CONN_PORT with the value as 8443, HTTPS_CERTIFICATE with the value as domain.crt or a self-signed certificate, and DOMAIN_PRIVATE_KEY with the value as domain.key or the private key that we created in the previous recipe.
- func helloWorld(w http.ResponseWriter, r *http.Request) { fmt.Fprintf(w, "Hello World!") }: This is a Go function that takes ResponseWriter and Request as input parameters and writes Hello World! on an HTTP response stream.

Next, we declared `main()` from where the program execution begins. As this method does a lot of things, let's understand it line by line:

- `http.HandleFunc("/", helloWorld)`: Here, we are registering the `helloWorld` function with the URL pattern `/` using `HandleFunc` of the `net/http` package, which means `helloWorld` gets executed, passing `(http.ResponseWriter, *http.Request)` as input to it whenever we access the HTTPS URL pattern `/`.

- `err := http.ListenAndServeTLS(CONN_HOST+":"+CONN_PORT, HTTPS_CERTIFICATE, DOMAIN_PRIVATE_KEY, nil)`: Here, we are calling `http.ListenAndServeTLS` to serve HTTPS requests that handle each incoming connection in a separate Goroutine. `ListenAndServeTLS` accepts four parameters—server address, SSL certificate, private key, and a handler. Here, we are passing the server address as `localhost:8443`, our self-signed certificate, private key, and handler as `nil`, which means we are asking the server to use `DefaultServeMux` as a handler.

- `if err != nil { log.Fatal("error starting https server : ", err) return}`: Here, we check whether there are any problems in starting the server. If there are, then log the error(s) and exit with a status code of 1.

Defining REST APIs and routes

While writing RESTful APIs, it's very common to authenticate the user before allowing them to access it. A prerequisite to authenticating the user is to create the API routes, which we will be covering in this recipe.

How to do it...

1. Install the `github.com/gorilla/mux` and `github.com/gorilla/handlers` packages using the `go get` command, as follows:

```
$ go get github.com/gorilla/mux
$ go get github.com/gorilla/handlers
```

2. Create `http-rest-api.go`, where we will define three routes—`/status`, `/get-token` and `/employees`—along with their handlers, as follows:

```go
package main
import
(
  "encoding/json"
  "log"
  "net/http"
  "os"
  "github.com/gorilla/handlers"
  "github.com/gorilla/mux"
)
const
(
  CONN_HOST = "localhost"
  CONN_PORT = "8080"
)
type Employee struct
{
  Id int `json:"id"`
  FirstName string `json:"firstName"`
  LastName string `json:"lastName"`
}
type Employees []Employee
var employees []Employee
func init()
{
  employees = Employees
  {
    Employee{Id: 1, FirstName: "Foo", LastName: "Bar"},
    Employee{Id: 2, FirstName: "Baz", LastName: "Qux"},
  }
}
func getStatus(w http.ResponseWriter, r *http.Request)
{
  w.Write([]byte("API is up and running"))
}
func getEmployees(w http.ResponseWriter, r *http.Request)
{
  json.NewEncoder(w).Encode(employees)
}
func getToken(w http.ResponseWriter, r *http.Request)
{
  w.Write([]byte("Not Implemented"))
}
func main()
```

```
{
  router := mux.NewRouter().StrictSlash(true)
  router.HandleFunc("/status", getStatus).Methods("GET")
  router.HandleFunc("/get-token", getToken).Methods("GET")
  router.HandleFunc("/employees", getEmployees).Methods("GET")
  err := http.ListenAndServe(CONN_HOST+":"+CONN_PORT,
  handlers.LoggingHandler(os.Stdout, router))
  if err != nil
  {
    log.Fatal("error starting http server : ", err)
    return
  }
}
```

3. Run the program with the following command:

```
$ go run http-rest-api.go
```

How it works...

Once we run the program, the HTTP server will start locally listening on port 8080.

Next, you could execute a GET request from the command line as:

```
$ curl -X GET http://localhost:8080/status
 API is up and running
```

This will give you the status of the REST API. You could execute a GET request from the command line as:

```
$ curl -X GET http://localhost:8080/employees
[{"id":1,"firstName":"Foo","lastName":"Bar"},{"id":2,"firstName":"Baz","lastName":"Qux"}]
```

This will give you a list of all the employees. We could try to get the access token through the command line as:

```
$ curl -X GET http://localhost:8080/get-token
```

We will get the **Not Implemented** message from the server.

Let's understand the program we have written:

- `import ("encoding/json" "log" "net/http" "os" "github.com/gorilla/handlers" "github.com/gorilla/mux")`: Here, we imported `github.com/gorilla/mux` to create a Gorilla Mux router and `github.com/gorilla/handlers` to create a Gorilla logging handler for logging HTTP requests in the Apache Common Log Format.

- `func getStatus(w http.ResponseWriter, r *http.Request) { w.Write([]byte("API is up and running")) }`: This is a handler that just writes **API is up and running** to an HTTP response stream.

- `func getEmployees(w http.ResponseWriter, r *http.Request) { json.NewEncoder(w).Encode(employees) }`: This is a handler that writes a static array of employees to an HTTP response stream.

- `func notImplemented(w http.ResponseWriter, r *http.Request) { w.Write([]byte("Not Implemented")) }`: This is a handler that just writes **Not Implemented** to an HTTP response stream.

- Then, we defined `main()`, where we create a `gorilla/mux` router instance using the `NewRouter()` handler with the trailing slash behavior for new routes as `true`, add routes and register handlers to it, and finally call `http.ListenAndServe` to serve HTTP requests which handle each incoming connection in a separate Goroutine. `ListenAndServe` accepts two parameters—the server address and the handler. Here, we are passing the server address as `localhost:8080` and the handler as Gorilla `LoggingHandler`, which logs HTTP requests in the Apache Common Log Format.

Creating a JSON web token

To secure your REST API or a service endpoint, you have to write a handler in Go that generates a JSON web token, or `JWT`.

In this recipe, we will be using `https://github.com/dgrijalva/jwt-go` to generate `JWT`, although you can implement any library from a number of third-party libraries available in Go, such as `https://github.com/square/go-jose` and `https://github.com/tarent/loginsrv`.

How to do it...

1. Install the `github.com/dgrijalva/jwt-go`, `github.com/gorilla/mux` and `github.com/gorilla/handlers` packages using the `go get` command, as follows:

```
$ go get github.com/dgrijalva/jwt-go
$ go get github.com/gorilla/handlers
$ go get github.com/gorilla/mux
```

2. Create `create-jwt.go`, where we will define the `getToken` handler that generates JWT, as follows:

```go
package main
import
(
  "encoding/json"
  "log"
  "net/http"
  "os"
  "time"
  jwt "github.com/dgrijalva/jwt-go"
  "github.com/gorilla/handlers"
  "github.com/gorilla/mux"
)
const
(
  CONN_HOST = "localhost"
  CONN_PORT = "8080"
  CLAIM_ISSUER = "Packt"
  CLAIM_EXPIRY_IN_HOURS = 24
)
type Employee struct
{
  Id int `json:"id"`
  FirstName string `json:"firstName"`
  LastName string `json:"lastName"`
}
type Employees []Employee
var employees []Employee
func init()
{
  employees = Employees
  {
    Employee{Id: 1, FirstName: "Foo", LastName: "Bar"},
    Employee{Id: 2, FirstName: "Baz", LastName: "Qux"},
```

```go
      }
  }
  var signature = []byte("secret")
  func getToken(w http.ResponseWriter, r *http.Request)
  {
    claims := &jwt.StandardClaims
    {
      ExpiresAt: time.Now().Add(time.Hour *
      CLAIM_EXPIRY_IN_HOURS).Unix(),
      Issuer: CLAIM_ISSUER,
    }
    token := jwt.NewWithClaims(jwt.SigningMethodHS256, claims)
    tokenString, _ := token.SignedString(signature)
    w.Write([]byte(tokenString))
  }
  func getStatus(w http.ResponseWriter, r *http.Request)
  {
    w.Write([]byte("API is up and running"))
  }
  func getEmployees(w http.ResponseWriter, r *http.Request)
  {
    json.NewEncoder(w).Encode(employees)
  }
  func main()
  {
    muxRouter := mux.NewRouter().StrictSlash(true)
    muxRouter.HandleFunc("/status", getStatus).Methods("GET")
    muxRouter.HandleFunc("/get-token", getToken).Methods("GET")
    muxRouter.HandleFunc("/employees", getEmployees).Methods("GET")
    err := http.ListenAndServe(CONN_HOST+":"+CONN_PORT,
    handlers.LoggingHandler(os.Stdout, muxRouter))
    if err != nil
    {
      log.Fatal("error starting http server : ", err)
      return
    }
  }
```

3. Run the program with the following command:

```
$ go run create-jwt.go
```

How it works...

Once we run the program, the HTTP server will start locally listening on port 8080.

Next, we execute a GET request from the command line as:

```
$ curl -X GET http://localhost:8080/status
 API is up and running
```

It will give you the status of the API. Next, we execute a GET request from the command line as:

```
$ curl -X GET http://localhost:8080/employees
[{"id":1,"firstName":"Foo","lastName":"Bar"},{"id":2,"firstName":"Baz","lastName":"Qux"}]
```

It will give you a list of all the employees. Next, let's attempt to get the access token of the REST API through the command line:

```
$ curl -X GET http://localhost:8080/get-token
```

It will give us the JWT token generated:

```
eyJhbGciOiJIUzI1NiIsInR5cCI6IkpXVCJ9.eyJleHAiOjE1MTM1MDY4ODEsImlzcyI6IlBhY2t0In0.95vuiR7lpWt4AIBDasBzOffL_Xv78_J9rcrKkeqSW08
```

Next, browse to `https://jwt.io/` and paste the token generated in the **Encoded** section to see it's decoded value, as shown in the following screenshot:

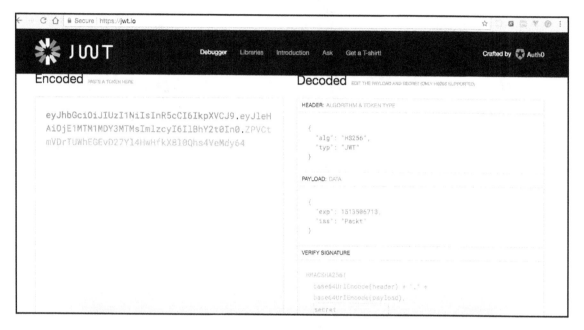

Let's understand the changes we introduced in this recipe:

- `import ( "encoding/json" "log" "net/http" "os" "time" jwt "github.com/dgrijalva/jwt-go" "github.com/gorilla/handlers" "github.com/gorilla/mux")`: Here, we imported an additional package—`github.com/dgrijalva/jwt-go`—which has a Go implementation of the JWT.

- `const ( CONN_HOST = "localhost" CONN_PORT = "8080" CLAIM_ISSUER = "Packt" CLAIM_EXPIRY_IN_HOURS = 24 )`: Here, we introduced two additional constants—one is `CLAIM_ISSUER`, which identifies the principal that issued the JWT, and the other one is `CLAIM_EXPIRY_IN_HOURS`, which identifies the expiration time on or after which the JWT must not be accepted for processing.

- `var signature = []byte("secret")`: This is the signature held by the server. Using this, the server will be able to verify existing tokens and sign new ones.

Next, we defined a `getToken` handler, where we first prepared a claims object using the JWT `StandardClaims` handler, which then generates a JWT token using the `jwt NewWithClaims` handler, and, finally, signs it with the server signature and writes it to an HTTP response stream.

Securing a RESTful service using a JSON web token

Once we have a REST API endpoint and a JWT token generator handler in hand, we can easily secure our endpoints with the JWT, which we will be covering in this recipe.

How to do it...

1. Install the `github.com/auth0/go-jwt-middleware`, `github.com/dgrijalva/jwt-go`, `github.com/gorilla/mux`, and `github.com/gorilla/handlers` packages using the `go get` command, as follows:

   ```
   $ go get github.com/auth0/go-jwt-middleware
   $ go get github.com/dgrijalva/jwt-go
   $ go get github.com/gorilla/handlers
   $ go get github.com/gorilla/mux
   ```

2. Create `http-rest-api-secured.go`, where we will define the JWT middleware to check for JWTs on HTTP requests, and wrap the `/employees` route with it, as follows:

   ```
   package main
   import
   (
     "encoding/json"
     "log"
     "net/http"
     "os"
     "time"
     jwtmiddleware "github.com/auth0/go-jwt-middleware"
     jwt "github.com/dgrijalva/jwt-go"
     "github.com/gorilla/handlers"
     "github.com/gorilla/mux"
   )
   ```

```go
const
(
  CONN_HOST = "localhost"
  CONN_PORT = "8080"
  CLAIM_ISSUER = "Packt"
  CLAIM_EXPIRY_IN_HOURS = 24
)
type Employee struct
{
  Id int `json:"id"`
  FirstName string `json:"firstName"`
  LastName string `json:"lastName"`
}
type Employees []Employee
var employees []Employee
func init()
{
  employees = Employees
  {
    Employee{Id: 1, FirstName: "Foo", LastName: "Bar"},
    Employee{Id: 2, FirstName: "Baz", LastName: "Qux"},
  }
}
var signature = []byte("secret")
var jwtMiddleware = jwtmiddleware.New
(
  jwtmiddleware.Options
  {
    ValidationKeyGetter: func(token *jwt.Token) (interface{},
error)
    {
      return signature, nil
    },
    SigningMethod: jwt.SigningMethodHS256,
  }
)
func getToken(w http.ResponseWriter, r *http.Request)
{
  claims := &jwt.StandardClaims
  {
    ExpiresAt: time.Now().Add(time.Hour *
    CLAIM_EXPIRY_IN_HOURS).Unix(),
    Issuer: CLAIM_ISSUER,
  }
  token := jwt.NewWithClaims(jwt.SigningMethodHS256, claims)
  tokenString, _ := token.SignedString(signature)
  w.Write([]byte(tokenString))
}
```

```
func getStatus(w http.ResponseWriter, r *http.Request)
{
  w.Write([]byte("API is up and running"))
}
func getEmployees(w http.ResponseWriter, r *http.Request)
{
  json.NewEncoder(w).Encode(employees)
}
func main()
{
  muxRouter := mux.NewRouter().StrictSlash(true)
  muxRouter.HandleFunc("/status", getStatus).Methods("GET")
  muxRouter.HandleFunc("/get-token", getToken).Methods("GET")
  muxRouter.Handle("/employees", jwtMiddleware.Handler
  (http.HandlerFunc(getEmployees))).Methods("GET")
  err := http.ListenAndServe(CONN_HOST+":"+CONN_PORT,
  handlers.LoggingHandler(os.Stdout, muxRouter))
  if err != nil
  {
    log.Fatal("error starting http server : ", err)
    return
  }
}
```

3. Run the program with the following command:

```
$ go run http-rest-api-secured.go
```

How it works...

Once we run the program, the HTTP server will start locally listening on port 8080.

Next, we execute a GET request from the command line as:

```
$ curl -X GET http://localhost:8080/status
 API is up and running
```

It will give you the status of the API. Next we execute a GET request from the command line as:

```
$ curl -X GET http://localhost:8080/employees
 Required authorization token not found
```

It will display us the message that the JWT was not found in the request. So, to get the list of all the employees, we have to get the access token of the API, which we can get by executing the following command:

```
$ curl -X GET http://localhost:8080/get-token

eyJhbGciOiJIUzI1NiIsInR5cCI6IkpXVCJ9.eyJleHAiOjE1MTM1MTI2NTksImlzcyI6IlBhY2
t0In0.2r_q_82erdOmt862ofluiMGr3O5x5_cO_sMyW7Pi5XE
```

Now, calling the employee API, again passing the JWT as the HTTP `Authorization` request header as:

```
$ curl -H "Authorization: Bearer
eyJhbGciOiJIUzI1NiIsInR5cCI6IkpXVCJ9.eyJleHAiOjE1MTM1MTI2NTksImlzcyI6IlBhY2
t0In0.2r_q_82erdOmt862ofluiMGr3O5x5_cO_sMyW7Pi5XE"
http://localhost:8080/employees
```

It will give you a list of all the employees, as follows:

```
[{"id":1,"firstName":"Foo","lastName":"Bar"},{"id":2,"firstName":"Baz","las
tName":"Qux"}]
```

Let's understand the changes we introduced in this recipe:

1. Using `import ("encoding/json" "log" "net/http" "os" "time"
   jwtmiddleware "github.com/auth0/go-jwt-middleware" jwt
   "github.com/dgrijalva/jwt-go" "github.com/gorilla/handlers"
   "github.com/gorilla/mux")`, we imported an additional
   package, `github.com/auth0/go-jwt-middleware`, with the alias as
   `jwtmiddleware`, which checks for JWTs on HTTP requests.
2. Then, we constructed a new secure instance of `jwtmiddleware`, passing
   `SigningMethod` as `HS256` and the `ValidationKeyGetter` option as a Go
   function that returns the key to validate the JWT. Here, a server signature is used
   as a key to validate the JWT.
3. Finally, we wrapped the `/employees` route with a `jwtmiddleware` handler
   in `main()`, which means for each request with the URL pattern `/employees`, we
   check and validate the JWT before serving the response.

Preventing cross-site request forgery in Go web applications

It's a common practice to secure web applications from a malicious website, email, blog, instant message, or a program attacking a trusted site for which the user is currently authenticated to prevent unwanted action. We often call this cross-site request forgery.

Implementing cross-site request forgery in Go is fairly easy using the Gorilla CSRF package, which we will be covering in this recipe.

How to do it...

1. Install the `github.com/gorilla/csrf` and `github.com/gorilla/mux` packages using the `go get` command, as follows:

```
$ go get github.com/gorilla/csrf
$ go get github.com/gorilla/mux
```

2. Create `sign-up.html` with name and email input text fields and an action that gets called whenever an HTML form is submitted, as follows:

```
<html>
  <head>
    <title>Sign Up!</title>
  </head>
  <body>
    <form method="POST" action="/post" accept-charset="UTF-8">
      <input type="text" name="name">
      <input type="text" name="email">
      {{ .csrfField }}
      <input type="submit" value="Sign up!">
    </form>
  </body>
</html>
```

3. Create `prevent-csrf.go`, where we create a `signUp` handler that renders a signup HTML form and a `post` handler that gets executed whenever an HTML form is submitted and the request has a valid CSRF token, as follows:

```go
package main
import
(
  "fmt"
  "html/template"
  "log"
  "net/http"
  "github.com/gorilla/csrf"
  "github.com/gorilla/mux"
)
const
(
  CONN_HOST = "localhost"
  CONN_PORT = "8443"
  HTTPS_CERTIFICATE = "domain.crt"
  DOMAIN_PRIVATE_KEY = "domain.key"
)
var AUTH_KEY = []byte("authentication-key")
func signUp(w http.ResponseWriter, r *http.Request)
{
  parsedTemplate, _ := template.ParseFiles("sign-up.html")
  err := parsedTemplate.Execute
  (
    w, map[string]interface{}
    {
      csrf.TemplateTag: csrf.TemplateField(r),
    }
  )
  if err != nil
  {
    log.Printf("Error occurred while executing the
    template : ", err)
    return
  }
}
func post(w http.ResponseWriter, r *http.Request)
{
  err := r.ParseForm()
  if err != nil
  {
    log.Print("error occurred while parsing form ", err)
  }
  name := r.FormValue("name")
```

```
      fmt.Fprintf(w, "Hi %s", name)
    }
    func main()
    {
      muxRouter := mux.NewRouter().StrictSlash(true)
      muxRouter.HandleFunc("/signup", signUp)
      muxRouter.HandleFunc("/post", post)
      http.ListenAndServeTLS(CONN_HOST+":"+CONN_PORT,
      HTTPS_CERTIFICATE, DOMAIN_PRIVATE_KEY, csrf.Protect
      (AUTH_KEY)(muxRouter))
    }
```

4. Run the program with the following command:

```
$ go run prevent-csrf.go
```

How it works...

Once we run the program, the HTTP server will start locally listening on port 8443.

Next, execute a POST request from the command line as:

```
$ curl -X POST --data "name=Foo&email=aggarwalarpit.89@gmail.com"
https://localhost:8443/post --insecure
```

It will give you the **Forbidden - CSRF token invalid** message as a response from the server and forbids you to submit an HTML form because the server does not find a valid CSRF token as part of the request:

```
→ ~ curl -X POST --data "name=Foo&email=aggarwalarpit.89@gmail.com" https://localhost:8443/post --insecure
Forbidden - CSRF token invalid
```

So, to submit a form, firstly we have to sign up, which generates a valid CSRF token by executing the following command:

```
$ curl -i -X GET https://localhost:8443/signup --insecure
```

This will give you an HTTP `X-CSRF-Token` , as shown in the following screenshot:

```
  $ curl -i -X GET https://localhost:8443/signup --insecure
HTTP/1.1 200 OK
Set-Cookie: _gorilla_csrf=MTUyMzQzMjg0OXxJa1ZLVTFsbGJHODFMMHg0VEdWc0wxZENVRVpCWVZGU1l6bHVMMVZKVEVVGM01EVjBUakVyUlVoTFFssVT1JZ289fJI5dumuyObaHVp97GN_CiZBCCpnbO0wlIwg5gvHL7-C; HttpOnly;
 Secure
Vary: Cookie
Date: Wed, 11 Apr 2018 07:47:29 GMT
Content-Length: 404
Content-Type: text/html; charset=utf-8

<html>
 <head>
 <title>Sign Up!</title>
 </head>
 <body>
  <form method="POST" action="/post" accept-charset="UTF-8">
  <input type="text" name="name">
  <input type="text" name="email">
   <input type="hidden" name="gorilla.csrf.Token" value="M9gqV7rRcXERv5JVR5YprcMzwtFmjEHKXRm6C8cDC4EjTLIt4OiNzVrHfYNB12nEx280rrKs8fqOgvfcJgQiFA==">
  <input type="submit" value="Sign up!">
  </form>
 </body>
</html>
```

And now you have to pass it as an HTTP `X-CSRF-Token` request header along with an HTTP cookie to submit an HTML form, as follows:

```
$ curl -X POST --data "name=Foo&email=aggarwalarpit.89@gmail.com" -H "X-
CSRF-Token:
M9gqV7rRcXERvSJVRSYprcMzwtFmjEHKXRm6C8cDC4EjTLIt4OiNzVrHfYNB12nEx280rrKs8fq
OgvfcJgQiFA==" --cookie
"_gorilla_csrf=MTUyMzQzMjg0OXxJa1ZLVTFsbGJHODFMMHg0VEdWc0wxZENVRVpCWVZGU1l6
bHVMMVZKVEVVGM01EVjBUakVyUlVoTFFssVT1JZ289fJI5dumuyObaHVp97GN_CiZBCCpnbO0wlIw
gSgvHL7-C;" https://localhost:8443/post --insecure

Hi Foo
```

Let's understand the program we have written:

- `const (CONN_HOST = "localhost" CONN_PORT = "8443" HTTPS_CERTIFICATE = "domain.crt" DOMAIN_PRIVATE_KEY = "domain.key")`: Here, we declared four constants - `CONN_HOST` with the value as `localhost`, `CONN_PORT` with the value as `8443`, `HTTPS_CERTIFICATE` with the value as `domain.crt` or a self-signed certificate, and `DOMAIN_PRIVATE_KEY` with the value as `domain.key` or the private key that we created in the previous recipe.
- `var AUTH_KEY = []byte("authentication-key")`: This is the authentication key which is used to generate the CSRF token.
- `signUp`: This is a handler that parses `sign-up.html` and provides an `<input>` field populated with a CSRF token replacing `{{ .csrfField }}` in the form.
- `post`: This is a handler that parses the submitted form, gets the value of the name input field, and writes it to an HTTP response stream.

Finally, we defined `main()`, where we create a `gorilla/mux` router instance using the `NewRouter()` handler with the trailing slash behavior for new routes as `true`, registered the `/signup` route with the `signUp` handler and the `/post` route with the `post` handler, and called the `http.ListenAndServeTLS` passing handler as `csrf.Protect(AUTH_KEY)(muxRouter)`, which makes sure all `POST` requests without a valid token will return `HTTP 403 Forbidden`.

11
Deploying a Go Web App and Docker Containers to AWS

In this chapter, we will cover the following recipes:

- Creating your first EC2 instance to run a Go web application
- Interacting with your first EC2 instance
- Creating, copying, and running a Go web application on your first EC2 instance
- Setting up an EC2 instance to run a Docker container
- Pulling a Docker image on an AWS EC2 instance from Docker Hub
- Running your Go Docker container on an EC2 instance

Introduction

Nowadays, every organization is moving toward DevOps and everyone is talking about continuous integration and continuous deployment, often termed as CI and CD, which have become must-have skills for developers to learn. When we refer to CI/CD, at a very high level, we talk about the deployment of containers to public/private clouds through continuous integration tools, such as Jenkins and Bamboo.

In this chapter, we will learn to deploy a simple Go web application and a Go Docker container to an EC2 instance provisioned manually. As we are going to work with Docker and AWS, I will assume you possess basic knowledge of Docker and AWS.

Creating your first EC2 instance to run a Go web application

Creating an EC2 instance on AWS is the same as getting a new machine and installing the required software to run a web application. In this recipe, we will create an EC2 instance, provision it, and run a simple Go web application.

Getting ready...

To start with the creating and deploying on an AWS EC2 instance, firstly, you have to create and activate an AWS account. Because this is out of context for this recipe, we will not be doing it here.

A well-explained process you can follow to create and activate an AWS account is available at `https://aws.amazon.com/premiumsupport/knowledge-center/create-and-act ivate-aws-account/`

How to do it...

1. Login into AWS, move to the **EC2 Management Console**, and click on **Launch Instance** in the **Create Instance** section, as shown in the following screenshot:

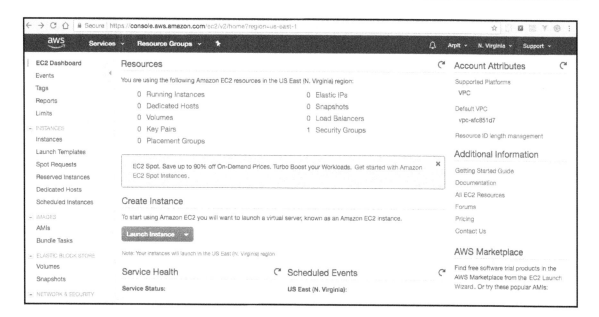

2. Select **Amazon Linux AMI 2017.09.1 (HVM), SSD Volume Type**, as shown in the following screenshot:

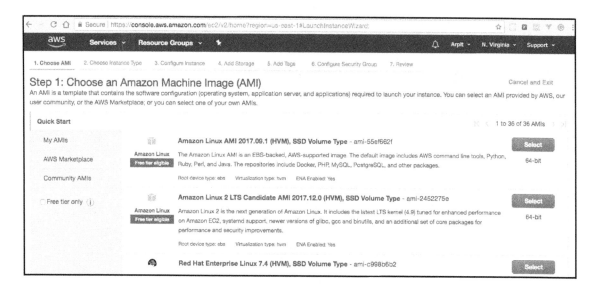

3. Select the **t2.micro** instance type and click on **Next: Configure Instance Details**:

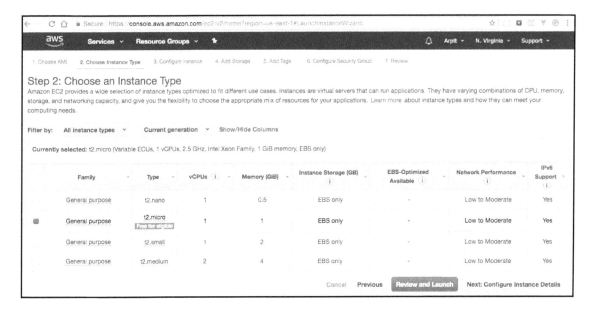

4. Enable **Auto-assign Public IP** in the **Configure Instance Details** section, as shown in the following screenshot:

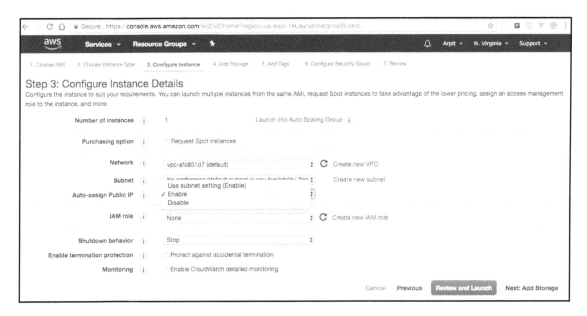

5. Do not make any changes to the **Add Storage** and **Add Tags** section.
6. Add the **HTTP** and **HTTPS** rule and click on the **Review and Launch** button in the **Configure Security Group** section, as shown in the following screenshot:

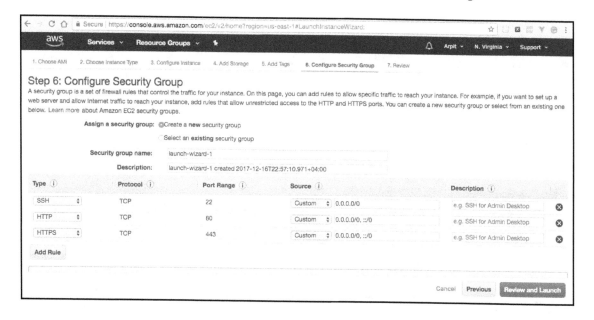

7. Select **Create a new key pair** from the drop-down menu, give a name to the key pair, and click on the **Download Key Pair** button. Save the `my-first-ec2-instance.pem` file and click on **Launch Instance**, as shown in the following screenshot:

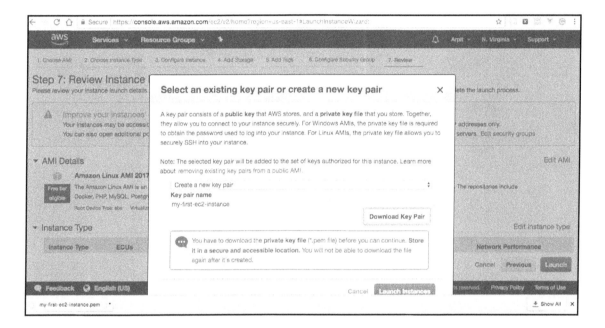

How it works...

Once you click on **Launch Instance**, it will create and boot up a Linux machine on AWS, assigning the instance an ID, public DNS, and public IP through which we can access it.

Moving to the **Instances** section of the **EC2 Dashboard**, you can see the instance running, as shown in the following screenshot:

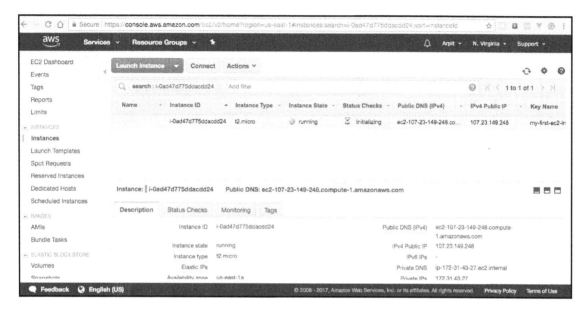

Interacting with your first EC2 instance

To deploy an application on an EC2 instance, we first have to login into it and install the necessary packages/software, which can be easily done through an `SSH` client, such as `MobaXterm`, `Putty`, and so on. In this recipe, we will login into an EC2 instance, which we created in the previous recipe, and install `Go` using the Red Hat package manager.

How to do it...

1. Set the permissions of the private key file—`my-first-ec2-instance.pem`—to `400`, which means the user/owner can read, can't write, and can't execute, whereas the group and others can't read, can't write, and can't execute it, by executing the `chmod` command, as follows:

```
$ chmod 400 my-first-ec2-instance.pem
```

2. Get the public DNS of the EC2 instance and connect to it using a private key file as an `ec2-user` by executing the `ssh` command, as follows:

```
$ ssh -i my-first-ec2-instance.pem ec2-
user@ec2-172-31-34-99.compute-1.amazonaws.com
```

Once the command has executed successfully, we will be logged in to the EC2 instance and the output will look like the following:

```
The authenticity of host 'ec2-54-196-74-162.compute-1.amazonaws.com (54.196.74.162)' can't be established.
RSA key fingerprint is 5e:88:cf:86:7c:38:d9:f5:a2:9d:f6:20:f4:e5:7c:2a.
Are you sure you want to continue connecting (yes/no)? yes
Warning: Permanently added 'ec2-54-196-74-162.compute-1.amazonaws.com,54.196.74.162' (RSA) to the list of known hosts.

       __|  __|_  )
       _|  (     /   Amazon Linux AMI
      ___|\___|___|

https://aws.amazon.com/amazon-linux-ami/2017.09-release-notes/
2 package(s) needed for security, out of 5 available
Run "sudo yum update" to apply all updates.
-bash: warning: setlocale: LC_CTYPE: cannot change locale (UTF-8): No such file or directory
[ec2-user@ip-172-31-34-99 ~]$
```

3. Switch to the `root` user from `ec2-user` by executing the `sudo` command:

```
[ec2-user@ip-172-31-34-99 ~]$ sudo su
```

4. Install Go using the Red Hat package manager, `yum`, as follows:

```
[root@ip-172-31-34-99 ~]$ yum install -y go
```

How it works...

Verify whether Go has been installed successfully for the `ec2-user` by executing the `go version` command, as follows:

```
[ec2-user@ip-172-31-34-99 ~]$ go version
go version go1.8.4 linux/amd64
```

Creating, copying, and running a Go web application on your first EC2 instance

Once we have an EC2 instance ready with the required libraries installed, we can simply copy the application using the secure copy protocol and then run it using the go run command, which we will be covering in this recipe.

How to do it...

1. Create http-server.go, where we will create a simple HTTP server that will render **Hello World!** browsing http://ec2-instance-public-dns:80 or executing curl -X GET http://ec2-instance-public-dns:80 from the command line, as follows:

```go
package main
import
(
  "fmt"
  "log"
  "net/http"
)
const
(
  CONN_PORT = "80"
)
func helloWorld(w http.ResponseWriter, r *http.Request)
{
  fmt.Fprintf(w, "Hello World!")
}
func main()
{
  http.HandleFunc("/", helloWorld)
  err := http.ListenAndServe(":"+CONN_PORT, nil)
  if err != nil
  {
    log.Fatal("error starting http server : ", err)
    return
  }
}
```

With everything in place, the directory structure should look like the following:

2. Copy `http-server.go` from the local machine directory to an EC2 user home (`/home/ec2-user`) directory using the secure copy or `scp` command, as follows:

```
$ scp -i my-first-ec2-instance.pem http-server.go ec2-
user@ec2-172-31-34-99.compute-1.amazonaws.com:/home/ec2-user
```

3. Login into an EC2 instance using a private key file and a public DNS name, as follows:

```
$ ssh -i my-first-ec2-instance.pem ec2-
user@ec2-172-31-34-99.compute-1.amazonaws.com
```

4. Run `http-server.go` in the background, executing the no hang-up or `nohup` command, as follows:

```
[ec2-user@ip-172-31-34-99 ~] $ nohup go run http-server.go &
```

How it works...

Once we run the program on an EC2 instance, the HTTP server will start locally listening on port `80`.

Next, execute a `GET` request from the command line as:

```
$ curl -i -X GET http://ec2-172-31-34-99.compute-1.amazonaws.com:80/
```

This will give **Hello World!** as a response, which will give the following output:

```
HTTP/1.1 200 OK
Date: Sat, 06 Jan 2018 10:59:38 GMT
Content-Length: 12
Content-Type: text/plain; charset=utf-8

Hello World!
```

Setting up an EC2 instance to run a Docker container

To run a Docker container on an EC2 instance, we first have to set up an instance with a Docker installation and add an `ec2-user` to the Docker group so that we can execute Docker commands with an `ec2-user` rather than as a `root` user, which we will be covering in this recipe.

How to do it...

1. Switch to the `root` user from the `ec2-user` user by executing the following command:

   ```
   [ec2-user@ip-172-31-34-99 ~]$ sudo su
   [root@ip-172-31-34-99 ec2-user]#
   ```

2. Install `Docker` and update an EC2 instance by executing the following commands:

   ```
   [root@ip-172-31-34-99 ec2-user] yum install -y docker
   [root@ip-172-31-34-99 ec2-user] yum update -y
   ```

3. Start `Docker` as a service on an EC2 instance by executing the following command:

   ```
   [root@ip-172-31-34-99 ec2-user] service docker start
   ```

4. Add `ec2-user` to the `docker` group so that you can execute Docker commands without using `sudo`, as follows:

   ```
   [root@ip-172-31-34-99 ec2-user] usermod -a -G docker ec2-user
   ```

5. Log out of the EC2 instance by executing the following commands:

```
[root@ip-172-31-34-99 ec2-user]# exit
 exit
[ec2-user@ip-172-31-34-99 ~]$ exit
 logout
Connection to ec2-172-31-34-99.compute-1.amazonaws.com closed.
```

6. Log in again to pick up the new Docker group permissions by executing the following command:

```
$ ssh -i my-first-ec2-instance.pem ec2-
user@ec2-172-31-34-99.compute-1.amazonaws.com
```

This will give us the output on the console, as shown in the following screenshot:

```
Last login: Wed Apr 11 06:12:24 2018 from 106.215.83.65

    __|  __|_  )
    _|  (     /    Amazon Linux AMI
   ___|\___|___|

https://aws.amazon.com/amazon-linux-ami/2017.09-release-notes/
9 package(s) needed for security, out of 15 available
Run "sudo yum update" to apply all updates.
-bash: warning: setlocale: LC_CTYPE: cannot change locale (UTF-8): No such file or directory
[ec2-user@ip-172-31-34-99 ~]$
```

How it works...

Login into an EC2 instance and verify whether `ec2-user` can run Docker commands without using `sudo` by executing following command:

```
[ec2-user@ip-54-196-74-162 ~]$ docker info
```

This will display system-wide information regarding the Docker installation, as shown in the following output:

```
Containers: 1
Running: 1
Paused: 0
Stopped: 0
Images: 1
...
Kernel Version: 4.9.62-21.56.amzn1.x86_64
Operating System: Amazon Linux AMI 2017.09
```

```
. . .
Live Restore Enabled: false
```

Pulling a Docker image on an AWS EC2 instance from Docker Hub

To run a Docker container, we need to have a Docker image, which we can either build from a `DockerFile` or can pull from any of the public or private Docker registries, such as Docker Hub, Quay, Google Container Registry, AWS Container Registry, and so on.

As we have already learned how to create a Docker image from a `DockerFile` and push it to Docker Hub in Chapter 9, *Working with Go and Docker*, we will not build an image again in this recipe. Instead, we will be pulling the pre-built image from Docker Hub on an EC2 instance.

 See the *Building your first Go Docker image* recipe in `Chapter 9`, *Working with Go and Docker*.

How to do it...

1. Login into Docker Hub using your credentials from the command line by executing the following command:

   ```
   $ docker login --username arpitaggarwal --password XXXXX
      Login Succeeded
   ```

2. Execute the `docker pull` command to pull `arpitaggarwal/golang-image` from Docker Hub, as follows:

```
$ docker pull arpitaggarwal/golang-image
```

This will result in the following output:

```
[ec2-user@ip-172-31-34-99 ~]$ docker pull arpitaggarwal/golang-image
Using default tag: latest
latest: Pulling from arpitaggarwal/golang-image
3e17c6eae66c: Pull complete
fdfb54153de7: Pull complete
a4ca6e73242a: Pull complete
93bd198d0a5f: Pull complete
2a43f474a764: Pull complete
e19893b2f35c: Pull complete
3b8a1a0cc426: Pull complete
85a9bedd68ab: Pull complete
7d686bba9845: Pull complete
2bb693dde155: Pull complete
Digest: sha256:c9e43c556581f4a1a741847d95af9aacd5a4e99f5fd68708f3e26cf88bac22a9
Status: Downloaded newer image for arpitaggarwal/golang-image:latest
[ec2-user@ip-172-31-34-99 ~]$
```

How it works...

Login into an EC2 instance and verify whether `arpitaggarwal/golang-image` has been pulled successfully from Docker Hub by executing the following command:

> `$ docker images`

This will list all the top-level images, their repositories, tags, and their size, as shown in the following screenshot:

```
[ec2-user@ip-172-31-34-99 ~]$ docker images
REPOSITORY                    TAG        IMAGE ID        CREATED         SIZE
arpitaggarwal/golang-image    latest     0bc234df2d2a    4 months ago    739MB
[ec2-user@ip-172-31-34-99 ~]$
```

Running your Go Docker container on an EC2 instance

Once we have a Docker image and Docker installed on an EC2 instance, then you can simply run the Docker container by executing the `docker run` command, which we will cover in this recipe.

How to do it...

Login into an EC2 instance and execute the `docker run` command to create and run a Docker container from `arpitaggarwal/golang-image`, assigning the container name as `golang-container`, using the `--name` flag, as follows:

```
$ docker run -d -p 80:8080 --name golang-container -it
arpitaggarwal/golang-image
   8a9256fcbffc505ad9406f5a8b42ae33ab3951fffb791502cfe3ada42aff781e
```

The `-d` flag specified in the `docker run` command starts the container in a daemon mode and the hash string at the end represents the ID of the `golang-container`.
The `-p` flag specified in the `docker run` command publishes a container's port(s) to the host. As we have an HTTP server running on port `8080` inside a Docker container and we opened port `80` for inbound traffic of our E2C instance, we mapped it as `80:8080`.

How it works...

Login into an EC2 instance and verify whether the Docker container has been created and is running successfully by executing the following command:

```
$ docker ps
```

Once the preceding command has executed successfully, it will give us the running Docker container details, as shown in the following screenshot:

```
[ec2-user@ip-172-31-34-99 ~]$ docker ps
CONTAINER ID   IMAGE                       COMMAND             CREATED        STATUS         PORTS                    NAMES
273b489403e8   arpitaggarwal/golang-image  "./arpitaggarwal"   9 seconds ago  Up 9 seconds   0.0.0.0:80->8080/tcp     golang-container
[ec2-user@ip-172-31-34-99 ~]$
```

Get the public DNS of an EC2 instance and execute a `GET` request from the command line as:

```
$ curl -i -X GET http://ec2-172-31-34-99.compute-1.amazonaws.com/
```

This will give **Hello World!** as a response, as shown in the following output:

```
HTTP/1.1 200 OK
Date: Sat, 06 Jan 2018 12:49:28 GMT
Content-Length: 12
Content-Type: text/plain; charset=utf-8
Hello World!
```

Other Books You May Enjoy

If you enjoyed this book, you may be interested in these other books by Packt:

Cloud Native programming with Golang
Mina Andrawos, Martin Helmich

ISBN: 978-1-78712-598-8

- Understand modern software applications architectures
- Build secure microservices that can effectively communicate with other services
- Get to know about event-driven architectures by diving into message queues such as Kafka, Rabbitmq, and AWS SQS.
- Understand key modern database technologies such as MongoDB, and Amazon's DynamoDB
- Leverage the power of containers
- Explore Amazon cloud services fundamentals
- Know how to utilize the power of the Go language to access key services in the Amazon cloud such as S3, SQS, DynamoDB and more.
- Build front-end applications using ReactJS with Go
  Implement CD for modern applications

Distributed Computing with Go
V.N. Nikhil Anurag

ISBN: 978-1-78712-538-4

- Gain proficiency with concurrency and parallelism in Go
- Learn how to test your application using Go's standard library
- Learn industry best practices with technologies such as REST, OpenAPI, Docker, and so on
- Design and build a distributed search engine
- Learn strategies on how to design a system for web scale

Leave a review - let other readers know what you think

Please share your thoughts on this book with others by leaving a review on the site that you bought it from. If you purchased the book from Amazon, please leave us an honest review on this book's Amazon page. This is vital so that other potential readers can see and use your unbiased opinion to make purchasing decisions, we can understand what our customers think about our products, and our authors can see your feedback on the title that they have worked with Packt to create. It will only take a few minutes of your time, but is valuable to other potential customers, our authors, and Packt. Thank you!

Index

error handling 88

www.ingramcontent.com/pod-product-compliance
Lightning Source LLC
Chambersburg PA
CBHW080621060326
40690CB00021B/4771